What Is
Christianity?

FORTRESS TEXTS IN MODERN THEOLOGY

What Is Christianity?

Adolf von Harnack

Translated by Thomas Bailey Saunders
Introduction by Rudolf Bultmann

Fortress Press   Philadelphia

FIRST FORTRESS PRESS EDITION 1986

Library of Congress Cataloging-in-Publication Data

Harnack, Adolf von, 1851-1930.
What is Christianity?

(Fortress texts in modern theology)
A collection of lectures given at the University of Berlin, 1899-1900.
Translation of: Das Wesen des Christentums.
Reprint.
Includes bibliographical references.
1. Christianity—Essence, genius, nature. I. Title.
II. Series.
BT60.H3713   1986   230   86-45209
ISBN 0-8006-3201-X

Printed in the United States of America   1-3201

94   93   92   91   90   2   3   4   5   6   7   8   9   10

CONTENTS

AUTHOR'S PREFACE TO THE
ENGLISH EDITION

To meet the wishes of my English friends I have assented to the publication of these Lectures in English as well as in German, and, as my esteemed friend Mr. Bailey Saunders was so self-denying and obliging as to undertake the translation of them, I was sure of their being in the best hands. Whether there is as great a need in England as there is in Germany for a short and plain statement of the Gospel and its history, I do not know. But this I know : the theologians of every country only half discharge their duties if they think it enough to treat of the Gospel in the recondite language of learning and bury it in scholarly folios.

A. HARNACK.

BERLIN, *October* 1900.

INTRODUCTION

by

RUDOLF BULTMANN

THE public lectures on "The Essence of Christianity"—
and here presented in English under the title *What is Christianity?*—were originally delivered at the University of
Berlin during the winter semester of 1899-1900, and made
their first appearance in book form in 1900. By 1927 the
volume had already been through fourteen printings and
had been translated into as many languages. At the beginning of our century it exerted an extraordinary influence
not only on the rising generation of theologians but also on
the educated classes generally. One can sense the impression the book created, both the enthusiastic acclaim and the
bitter antagonism with which it was received, by reading
the biography of Harnack issued in 1936 by his daughter,
Dr. Agnes von Zahn-Harnack.[1]

Today the echoes of this excitement are heard no more,
and few are the theological students who have even read
this book, once so famous and controversial. And now it is
appearing in a new edition. One might ask: Why, with what
justification?

The first and most important answer to this question is
that Harnack's book is a theological-historical document of
the greatest importance. Every theologian who would be
clear about the present situation in theology and its origins

---

[1] Agnes von Zahn-Harnack, *Adolf von Harnack,* pp. 242 ff. See
also the discussion occasioned by Harnack's book, *What is Christianity?* in the *Christliche Welt* for 1901 and the *Theologischer
Jahresbericht* for 1901 and 1902.

should be familiar with it. It should, moreover, be a part of required theological training and education.

The young theologian may also learn something else from this book; namely, what conceptions of Christianity he may presuppose to be current among the broad circles of the educated and semi-educated laymen to whom he must address his sermons and teachings. There is no doubt that the popular understanding of the Christian faith, insofar as in certain circles it does not bear the impress of traditional orthodoxy and pietism, accords in some measure with the portrait drawn by Harnack, even if it does not achieve his earnestness and subtlety. But it should also be stressed that this understanding of Christianity, although one may label it "liberal," is in no wise a lifeless residue of a vanished era which no longer needs to be taken seriously. On the contrary this "liberal" understanding, at the very least, contains active impulses which though now obscured nonetheless preserve their legitimacy and will recover their validity.

During a discussion on Protestant religious instruction, sponsored by the publication *Die Sammlung*,[2] Rudolph Lennert, in an open letter to Helmut Kittel, declared that "theologians, even perhaps in their own interests, must arrange to come to terms with these old concerns of liberal theology and in a manner somewhat more serious than they show today. For unless all signs are deceiving, these concerns will present themselves afresh to theologians with a new vigor, and with a new radicalism, as though strengthened by their long repose." One might also properly point out to those who would simply dismiss theological liberalism as a "false doctrine" that there is no heresy whose motivation and strength do not spring from a valid impulse that fails to achieve legitimate expression in the official "true doctrine," even when it seeks to wrest this acknowledgment of its worth by taking the path of error.

This, of course, is tantamount to saying that Harnack's

[2] *Die Sammlung*, 3 Jahrg, Nr. 11, Nov., 1948, p. 698.

What is Christianity? is to be read not only as a historic document, but also as a contribution to contemporary theological discussion. This would be the case even if the effective themes of this book were devoid of immediate import and even if they were not on the verge of coming into their own. For they are ever present as a possibility and therefore ever to be borne in mind.

Karl Barth rightly says that the task of theology cannot consist merely "in the establishment and transmission of the results already achieved in this or that classical period." Rather must theology "consist of an ever-renewed reflection." For just this reason must theology perform its task "in full earnestness again and again, indeed beginning from the beginning. But while this task is being performed, the theology of former times, be it classical or less than classical, also speaks to us and will be heard. . . ." In regard to theology we cannot be in the Church without confronting responsibly the theology of antiquity as well as that of the present. Augustine, Thomas, Luther, Schleiermacher, and all the others are not dead, but alive. There are heretics only in a relative sense and for this reason even those who are always viewed and judged as such, with all their recognized folly and wickedness, should and must have a voice in theology. The theology of every age must be sufficiently strong and free to hear, calmly, attentively, and openly, not only the voices of the Church Fathers, not only the voices of its favorites, not only the voices of classical antiquity, but all the voices of the past in its entirety. We cannot prescribe who among the collaborators of the past will be welcomed to participate in our own work, and who will not be. For there is always the possibility that in one sense or another we may be in particular need of wholly unexpected voices, and that among them there may be voices which are at first entirely unwelcome."[3] In my opinion Adolf Har-

[3] Karl Barth, *Die protestantische Theologie im 19. Jahrhundert,* 1947, pp. 2 ff.

nack also belongs to those "others" who are not dead but alive. And in view of the present danger of a new orthodoxy, and of the restoration of a narrow denominationalism, it is necessary that his voice not die out for the very reason that he belongs to those "disquieting figures" among whom Wilhelm Dilthey had included him in a letter to Count Yorck von Wartenburg.[4]

It goes without saying that today we canont read Harnack's *What Is Christianity?* without criticism. Precisely because it is to be hoped that the book will again be read with profit, the way must be cleared for its desired success by making some critical observations in advance.

It was a weakness of Harnack, dominated as he was by the new approach which had been opened to him by his study of the dogmas of the early church, that he failed to realize the importance of the so-called religious-historical school, and never truly became sympathetic to it. This is quite clear in his conception and presentation of the message of Jesus. Harnack somehow never clearly saw nor understood the eschatological character of the appearance of Jesus and of his preaching of the imminent advent of the Kingdom of God.[5] Moreover, Harnack never gave due consideration to the eschatological consciousness with which the early Christian communities and Paul were suffused. In fact, Harnack never even caught a glimpse of the utter strangeness of the image of primitive Christianity disclosed by the religious-historical school, and which even today at first inevitably shocks a reader of the New Testament.

Harnack evidently never experienced such a reaction of

[4]*Briefwechsel zwischen Wilhelm Dilthey und dem Grafen Paul Yorck von Wartenburg, 1877-97* (1923), p. 231.

[5] Cf. Albert Schweitzer, *Geschichte der Leben-Jesu-Forschung*, 1913, p. 246: "In his *What is Christianity?* Harnack almost entirely neglects the specific historical setting and stamp of the doctrine of Jesus and he concerns himself with only one Gospel, through which he comes to year 1899 without any trouble." (*Ed. note:* The English translation is published as *The Quest of the Historical Jesus*, New York, Macmillan, 1954.)

shock. As a result he diluted to the point of harmlessness, as it were, the ever-problematical core of Christianity, of which Kierkegaard, who did not need any such religious-historical lesson, bore the full brunt. The problem is simply this: how is a Christian existence possible in this world when one, in both his work and pleasures, shares in its culture, its tasks, and its worldly goods? It would appear that for Harnack the reconciliation of the Christian with the Goethian conception of the world created no great difficulties. Hence it is quite easy to see that despite all his efforts —a modern reader might even describe them as moving— Harnack possessed no "antennae" for the theology of Karl Barth.[6] Can the paradoxical situation of primitive Christianity hovering "between the times"—that is between the "old" and the "new aeon"—be at all viewed as valid after the eschatalogical expectations of the first Christian generations were extinguished? Is Christian life, perceived and prescribed in the New Testament as a "transcendental" life, viable? The author of *What is Christianity?* was never worried by such questions—curiously enough, one is tempted to say today—and it is characteristic of him that the Pauline "as though not" (1 Cor. 7:29-31)[7] played no role in his thought.

Consequently, even in his history of church dogma, the problem of the stormy disputes that raged over the reconciliation of the early church with the indefinite postponement of the end of the world and the coming of Christ was never posed or discussed in valid terms. (Recently, Martin

---

[6] See Agnes von Harnack's biography, p. 543 and especially p. 532, on the discussion between Harnack and Barth.

[7] *Ed. note:* The Revised Standard Version reads: "I mean, brethren, the appointed time has grown very short; from now on, let those who have wives live as though they had none, and those who mourn as though they were not mourning, and those who rejoice as they they were not rejoicing, and those who buy as though they had no goods, and those who deal with the world as though they had no dealings with it. For the form of this world is passing away."

Werner has dealt with this problem from an opposite point of view. Despite its character of one-sidedness valid observations are brought to bear on the question.[8]) Harnack's limited treatment of this problem is closely linked to his one-sided understanding of Gnosticism which he described as an "acute Hellenization" of the Gospel.[9] His interest centered on the Gnostic systems which had arisen on Greek soil, and which in their development partly used the resources of Greek thought. Neither the pre-Christian (Oriental) origin of Gnosticism, nor the motives distinctive to it, came into Harnack's historical perspective. This means, however, that he misunderstood the peculiar parallelism resting on a sense of the problematic character that the world had assumed for the adherents of both movements, and on a conception that the true Self of man and his real existence were in radical opposition to all other Being imprisoned in the forms of this world. The real differences between the answers given to the questions which arose out of the posing of an analogous problem were never more clearly expressed by Harnack.

To be sure, we are today sensitive to such a limitation of the historical and, therefore, the systematic understanding of Christianity. It is in truth one of the pranks of history, as Harnack himself often observed with a smile, that his de-emphasis of the eschatological problem to the point of rendering it harmless is especially appealing to the very persons who are otherwise little disposed to accept the outlook of *What is Christianity?* But no matter how acutely aware we may be of Harnack's limitations it would be too simple to say that he had no ear for that in the New Testament message which is transcendental, and which calls out to men to detach themselves from the "world." Harnack's

[8] Martin Werner, *Die Enstehung des Christlichen Dogmas*, 1941.
[9] This question was raised by W. Bousset in his review of Harnack's book in the *Theologische Rundschau*, IV, 1901, pp. 102 ff. See also the polemic of Hans Jonas against Harnack in his *Gnosis und Spätantiker Geist,* I, 1934, pp. 49 ff.

only fault was that he neglected to bring the message to the surface of consciousness explicitly and in all its radicalism. Here one point should be made before all else. Despite the fact that Harnack undertook the task of describing the "essence of Christianity" in the spirit of a historian primarily, he nonetheless never portrayed the *essence itself* as a historical phenomenon. To Harnack the question of "essence" was at one and the same time the question of its actuality and its present validity. He seemed not to realize clearly, however, that he could not deal adequately with precisely these features because of his exclusive reliance on the inductive method that he thought he was following.

In truth, Harnack's procedure of abstracting the essence from the total history of Christianity was methodologically legitimate in intention. That is to say that he let the history of Christianity define those questions whose very formulation, in the first instance and most completely, discloses the nature of its origins. Though his conception of history is otherwise dominated to a great extent by the idea of evolution—the optimism of this faith in evolution has become questionable in our time—it is nevertheless quite clear that for him the Christian faith is neither a product of evolution, nor, as such, something with a history subject to development. Since Harnack evaluated all the phenomena of church history in terms of the original Gospel, it therefore never occurred to him that the contemporary Christian faith necessarily had to go beyond the Reformation in which the original meaning of the Gospel had been rediscovered.

Harnack characterizes the Christian faith, which he was wont to call the "Christian religion," as "something simple and sublime" which means "one thing and one thing only," and as "eternal life in the midst of time, by the strength and under the eyes of God." He did this because Christian faith relates to man "as one who in the midst of all change and progress himself never changes." This is a decisive characterization. According to it, the Christian faith views

the innermost Self and Being of man as differentiated from
the world and raises him above it. "It is a supernatural
element alone that ever enables us to get at the meaning of
life; for natural existence ends in death. . . . But here the
kingdom of God, the Eternal, entered into time." . . . "The
powers of the Gospel appeal to the deepest foundations of
human existence and to them only." . . . "Either that is
nonsense—namely, the statement of Jesus that even the
hairs on our heads are numbered—or else it is the utmost
development of which religion is capable; no longer a mere
phenomenon accompanying the life of the senses, a coefficient, a transfiguration of certain parts of that life, but
something which sets up a paramount title to be the first
and the only fact that reveals the fundamental basis and
meaning of life. Religion subordinates to itself the whole
motley world of phenomena, and defies that world if it
claims to be the only real one. Religion gives us only a single
experience, but one which presents the world in a new light:
the Eternal appears; time becomes means to an end; man
is seen to be on the side of the Eternal."

It may be helpful to review the well-known formulations
of Harnack which were under attack in the light of these
statements: "In the combination of these ideas—God the
father, Providence, the position of men as God's children,
the infinite value of the human soul—the whole Gospel is
expressed," or his "God and the soul, the soul and its
God." It must be apparent that despite the incompleteness
of the formulation Harnack's aim is to express the unworldi-
ness of Christian existence. This is further shown by the
posing of the decisive alternatives: ". . . God or Mammon,
an eternal or an earthly life, the soul or the body, humility
or self-righteousness, love or selfishness, truth or falsehood.
The sphere which these questions occupy is all-embracing;
the individual is called upon to listen to the glad message
of mercy and the Fatherhood of God, and to make up his
mind whether he will be on the side of God and the Eternal,

or on the side of the world and of time. . . . The Gospel
rests on the conflict between the flesh and the spirit, God
and the world, good and evil."

It is thereby seen quite clearly that Christian existence
can be achieved neither by actively changing the world, nor
by asceticism. The Gospel does not demand asceticism, but
a struggle against Mammon, care, and selfishness. The Sermon on the Mount does not demand the renunciation of
law in general, but the individual renunciation of the pursuit of one's rights in opposition to one's fellow man. Neither
is the Gospel a social message nor the basis of a political
program. But it does summon all men to hearken to their
responsibilities in all spheres of life. It is quite characteristic
for Harnack to make the following comment on 1 John 2:17:
"We have to do with a dualism which arose we know not
how; but as moral beings we are convinced that, as it has
been given us in order that we may overcome it in ourselves
and bring it to a unity, and will at last find its reconciliation
in the great far-off event, the realized dominion of the
Good."

Naturally this view is open to criticism. However, one
thing must be seen here; namely, that the difference between
faith and a "world-view" finds expression. Harnack's failure
to formulate this distinction more lucidly rests on the fact
that he did not clearly see the difference between the
kerygmatic ("proclamatory")[10] character of the Gospel and
an "Enlightenment" doctrine or an ethical appeal. This very
failure is responsible for the fragmentary character of his
Christological views.

If Harnack's statement that "the Gospel has to do with
the Father only, not the Son, as Jesus proclaimed," at one

[10] Ed. note: The Greek noun kerygma is perhaps the most distinctive term in current theological discussion and study. Related
to the word keryx (herald), it means "a proclamation"; in the
Gospels and the Epistles of Paul where it is observed to play a
central role, it implies the proclamation of the Christian message
of salvation.

time provoked a considerable affront it was only because the words "as Jesus proclaimed" were blithely overlooked: "It is not as a mere component that he is connected with the Gospel; he was its personal realization and its strength, and this he is felt to be still." There is no denying this: if one understands the Gospel (according to these citations) as a collection of statements reflecting the message of the historical Jesus—statements indeed which encourage characterization as "doctrine"—then Jesus certainly does not belong within the Gospel. He is not a component part, he is the whole—and this is what is striving to be said, however imperfectly, in that other statement of Harnack's.

Harnack's polemic against the traditional Church Christology is to this extent fully justified. The latter indeed commits the decisive error of developing Christianity as a "doctrine." Only Christ can give the kerygmatic character to everything which is "taught" as Christian. It is only Christ who transfigures the doctrine into kerygma. Therefore, Christ is correctly preached not where something is said *about* him, but only where he himself becomes the proclaimer. Harnack should have, at least, made an effort to conceive of Christ from this standpoint. But at the same time as he rejects the Christology of the Church he also cuts off the escape route of those who complain about the incomprehensibility of Christology. They do this in order to escape submitting to the words of Jesus: "No!" Harnack says, "his message is simpler than the churches would like to think it, simpler, but for that very reason sterner and endowed with a greater claim to universality. A man cannot evade it by the subterfuge of saying: 'I can make nothing of this "Christology," therefore, this sermon is not for me.' "

In his justified polemic against a false understanding of the "true doctrine" and his equally justified struggle for freedom against enforced doctrinal conformity, it must be said that Harnack could hardly have reflected deeply upon the legitimate meaning of the doctrine of the Christian church. And therein lay one of his major weaknesses which Count Yorck has correctly perceived. In a criticism of Harnack's study of the history of church dogma, he objected to the "localization of religion outside the intellect" as savoring of Schleiermacher; and Yorck commented reproachfully: "Dogmatics is presented as a process in the deterioration of religion." And Yorck is further of the opinion: "Here one misses the neglected philosopher, that is, psychologist [Yorck was, naturally, referring to the so-called 'understanding' psychology of Dilthey] who can establish and explain the inevitable connections of feeling, imagination and representation."[11] Is this, however, only the task of philosophers or psychologists? Or is it not also the task of theologians—indeed, theirs above all? Must not the "true doctrine" be developed from an analysis of the necessity of faith and the meaning of dogmatics? The latter need not have the same meaning, to be sure, as *the* church dogmatics against which Harnack's polemic was directed.

As an understandable reaction against a neo-orthodoxy— be it a restoration of denominationalism or a vulgarized "Barthianism"—there is today a resurgence of "liberalism" within the Church. This movement too should be wary of becoming a mere reversion to a pristine state ("repristination"): otherwise it will be guilty of badly administering Harnack's heritage. For if we now treat Harnack's *What is Christianity?* as a compendium of true doctrine, we would be acting against his very spirit. We will remain true to Harnack only if we appropriate his legacy critically. True loyalty is never an "archaizing repetition," but only a critical appropriation which makes the legitimate impulses of tradition its very own and endows these emphases with validity in a new form.

It is the hope that this new edition should serve to keep

---

[11] *Briefwechsel zwischen . . . Dilthey und. . . . Yorck,* 109.

alive the memory of the legitimate motives realized in Harnack's *What is Christianity?* and to restore to them their
rightful place in contemporary discussion.[12]

Translated by Salvator Attanasio and Ephraim Fischoff.

---

[12] *Ed. note:* The original of this essay is signed "Marburg, early
in 1950" and appeared as the introduction to the new edition
which was issued by the Ehrenfried Klotz Verlag in Stuttgart on
the occasion of the fiftieth anniversary of the original publication
of *What is Christianity?*

WHAT IS CHRISTIANITY?

LECTURE I.

THE great English philosopher, John Stuart Mill,
has somewhere observed that mankind cannot be too
often reminded that there was once a man of the
name of Socrates. That is true; but still more important is it to remind mankind again and again that
a man of the name of Jesus Christ once stood in their
midst. The fact, of course, has been brought home
to us from our youth up; but unhappily it cannot be
said that public instruction in our time is calculated
to keep the image of Jesus Christ before us in any impressive way, and make it an inalienable possession
after our school-days are over and for our whole life.
And although no one who has once absorbed a ray of
Christ's light can ever again become as though he had
never heard of him; although at the bottom of every
soul that has been once touched an impression remains,
a confused recollection of this kind, which is often only
a " superstitio," is not enough to give strength and
life. But where the demand for further and more

trustworthy knowledge about him arises, and a man wants positive information as to who Jesus Christ was, and as to the real purport of his message, he no sooner asks for it than he finds himself, if he consults the literature of the day, surrounded by a clatter of contradictory voices. He hears some people maintaining that primitive Christianity was closely akin to Buddhism, and he is accordingly told that it is in fleeing the world and in pessimism that the sublime character of this religion and its profound meaning are revealed. Others, on the contrary, assure him that Christianity is an optimistic religion, and that it must be thought of simply and solely as a higher phase of Judaism; and these people also suppose that in saying this they have said something very profound. Others, again, maintain the opposite; they assert that the Gospel did away with Judaism, but itself originated under Greek influences of mysterious operation; and that it is to be understood as a blossom on the tree of Hellenism. Religious philosophers come forward and declare that the metaphysical system which, as they say, was developed out of the Gospel is its real kernel and the revelation of its secret; but others reply that the Gospel has nothing to do with philosophy, that it was meant for feeling and suffering humanity, and that philosophy has only been forced upon it. Finally, the latest critics that have come into the field assure us that the whole history of religion, morality, and philosophy, is nothing but wrapping and ornament; that what at all times underlies them, as the only real motive power, is the history of economics; that, accordingly, Christianity, too, was in its origin nothing more than a social movement and Christ a social deliverer, the deliverer of the oppressed lower classes.

There is something touching in the anxiety which everyone shows to rediscover himself, together with his own point of view and his own circle of interest, in this Jesus Christ, or at least to get a share in him. It is the perennial repetition of the spectacle which was seen in the "Gnostic" movement even as early as the second century, and which takes the form of a struggle, on the part of every conceivable tendency of thought, for the possession of Jesus Christ. Why, quite recently, not only, I think, Tolstoi's ideas, but even Nietzsche's, have been exhibited in their special affinity with the Gospel; and there is perhaps more to be said even upon this subject that is worth attention than upon the connexion between a good deal of "theological" and "philosophical" speculation and Christ's teaching.

But nevertheless, when taken together, the impression which these contradictory opinions convey is disheartening: the confusion seems hopeless. How can we take it amiss of anyone, if, after trying to find out how the question stands, he gives it up? Perhaps he goes further, and declares that after all the question does not matter. How are we concerned with events that happened, or with a person who lived, nineteen hundred years ago? We must look for our ideals and our strength to the present; to evolve them laboriously out of old manuscripts is a fantastic proceeding that can lead nowhere. The man who so speaks is not wrong; but neither is he right. What we are and what we possess, in any high sense, we possess from the past and by the past—only so much of it, of course, as has had results and makes its influence felt up to the present day. To acquire a sound knowledge of the past is the business and the duty not only of the historian but also of every one who wishes to make the wealth and the strength so gained his own. But that the Gospel is a part of this past which nothing else can replace has been affirmed again and again by the greatest minds. "Let intellectual and spiritual culture progress, and the human mind expand, as much as it will; beyond the grandeur and the moral elevation of Christianity, as it sparkles and shines in the Gospels, the human mind will not advance." In these words Goethe, after making many experiments and labouring indefatigably at himself, summed up the result to which his moral and historical insight had led him. Even though we were to feel no desire on our own part, it would still be worth while, because of this man's testimony, to devote our serious attention to what he came to regard as so precious; and if, contrary to his declaration, louder and more confident voices are heard to-day, proclaiming that the Christian religion has outlived itself, let us accept that as an invitation to make a closer acquaintance with this religion whose certificate of death people suppose that they can already exhibit.

But in truth this religion and the efforts which it evokes are more active to-day than they used to be. We may say to the credit of our age that it takes an eager interest in the problem of the nature and value of Christianity, and that there is more search and inquiry in regard to this subject now than was the case thirty years ago. Even in the experiments that are made in and about it, the strange and abstruse replies that are given to questions, the way in which it is caricatured, the chaotic confusion which it exhibits, nay even in the hatred that it excites, a real life and an earnest endeavour may be traced. Only do not let us suppose that there is anything exemplary in this endeavour, and that we are the first who, after shaking off an authoritative religion, are struggling after one that shall really make us free and be of independent growth—a struggle which must of necessity give rise to much confusion and half-truth. Sixty-two years ago Carlyle wrote :— " In these distracted times, when the Religious Principle, driven out of most Churches, either lies unseen in the hearts of good men, looking and longing and silently working there towards some new Revelation ; or else wanders homeless over the world, like a disembodied soul seeking its terrestrial organisation, — into how many strange shapes, of

Superstition and Fanaticism, does it not tentatively and errantly cast itself! The higher Enthusiasm of man's nature is for the while without Exponent; yet does it continue indestructible, unweariedly active, and work blindly in the great chaotic deep : thus Sect after Sect, and Church after Church, bodies itself forth, and melts again into new metamorphosis."

No one who understands the times in which we live can deny that these words sound as if they had been written to-day. But it is not with "the religious principle" and the ways in which it has developed that we are going to concern ourselves in these lectures. We shall try to answer the more modest but not less pressing question, What is Christianity? What was it? What has it become? The answer to this question may, we hope, also throw light by the way on the more comprehensive one, What is Religion, and what ought it to be to us? In dealing with religion, is it not after all with the Christian religion alone that we have to do? Other religions no longer stir the depths of our hearts.

What is Christianity? It is solely in its historical sense that we shall try to answer this question here; that is to say, we shall employ the methods of historical science, and the experience of life gained by studying the actual course of history. This excludes the view of the question taken by the apologist and the religious philosopher. On this point permit me to say a few words.

Apologetics holds a necessary place in religious knowledge, and to demonstrate the validity of the Christian religion and exhibit its importance for the moral and intellectual life is a great and a worthy undertaking. But this undertaking must be kept quite separate from the purely historical question as to the nature of that religion, or else historical research will be brought into complete discredit. Moreover, in the kind of apologetics that is now required no really high standard has yet been attained. Apart from a few steps that have been taken in the direction of improvement, apologetics as a subject of study is in a deplorable state : it is not clear as to the positions to be defended, and it is uncertain as to the means to be employed. It is also not infrequently pursued in an undignified and obtrusive fashion. Apologists imagine that they are doing a great work by crying up religion as though it were a job-lot at a sale, or a universal remedy for all social ills. They are perpetually snatching, too, at all sorts of baubles, so as to deck out religion in fine clothes. In their endeavour to present it as a glorious necessity, they deprive it of its earnest character, and at the best only prove that it is something which may be safely accepted because it can do no harm. Finally, they cannot refrain from slipping in some church programme of yesterday and " demonstrating " its claims as well. The structure of their ideas is so loose that an idea or two more makes no difference. The mischief that has been thereby

done already and is still being done is indescribable.
No! the Christian religion is something simple and
sublime; it means one thing and one thing only:
Eternal life in the midst of time, by the strength and
under the eyes of God.   It is no ethical or social *ar-
canum* for the preservation or improvement of things
generally.   To make what it has done for civilisation
and human progress the main question, and to determine its value by the answer, is to do it violence
at the start.   Goethe once said, "Mankind is always
advancing, and man always remains the same."   It is
to *man* that religion pertains, to man, as one who in
the midst of all change and progress himself never
changes.   Christian apologetics must recognise, then,
that it is with religion in its simple nature and its
simple strength that it has to do.   Religion, truly,
does not exist for itself alone, but lives in an inner
fellowship with all the activities of the mind and
with moral and economical conditions as well.   But
it is emphatically not a mere function or an exponent
of them ; it is a mighty power that sets to work of
itself, hindering or furthering, destroying or making
fruitful.   The main thing is to learn what religion
is and in what its essential character consists ; no
matter what position the individual who examines it
may take up in regard to it, or whether in his own
life he values it or not.

But the point of view of the philosophical theorist,
in the strict sense of the word, will also find no place
in these lectures.   Had they been delivered sixty

years ago, it would have been our endeavour to try to arrive by speculative reasoning at some general conception of religion, and then to define the Christian religion accordingly. But we have rightly become sceptical about the value of this procedure. *Latet dolus in generalibus.* We know to-day that life cannot be spanned by general conceptions, and that there is no general conception of religion to which actual religions are related simply and solely as species to genus. Nay, the question may even be asked whether there is any such generic conception as "religion" at all. Is the common element in it anything more than a vague disposition? Is it only an empty place in our innermost being that the word denotes, which every one fills up in a different fashion and many do not perceive at all? I am not of this opinion; I am convinced, rather, that at bottom we have to do here with something which is common to us all, and which in the course of history has struggled up out of torpor and discord into unity and light. I am convinced that Augustine is right when he says, " Thou, Lord, hast made us for Thyself, and our heart is restless until it finds rest in Thee." But to prove that this is so ; to exhibit the nature and the claims of religion by psychological analysis, including the psychology of peoples, is not the task that we shall undertake in what follows. We shall keep to the purely historical theme : What is the Christian religion?

Where are we to look for our materials? The answer seems to be simple and at the same time exhaustive : Jesus Christ and his Gospel. But however little doubt there may be that this must form not only our point of departure but also the matter with which our investigations will mainly deal, it is equally certain that we must not be content to exhibit the mere image of Jesus Christ and the main features of his Gospel. We must not be content to stop there, because every great and powerful personality reveals a part of what it is only when seen in those whom it influences. Nay, it may be said that the more powerful the personality which a man possesses, and the more he takes hold of the inner life of others, the less can the sum-total of what he is be known only by what he himself says and does. We must look at the reflection and the effects which he produced in those whose leader and master he became. That is why a complete answer to the question, What is Christianity, is impossible so long as we are restricted to Jesus Christ's teaching alone. We must include the first generation of his disciples as well—those who ate and drank with him—and we must listen to what they tell us of the effect which he had upon their lives.

But even this does not exhaust our materials. If Christianity is an example of a great power valid not for one particular epoch alone ; if in and through it, not once only, but again and again, great forces have been disengaged, we must include all the later products of its spirit. It is not a question of a " doctrine " being handed down by uniform repetition or arbitrarily distorted ; it is a question of a *life*, again and again kindled afresh, and now burning with a flame of its own. We may also add that Christ himself and the apostles were convinced that the religion which they were planting would in the ages to come have a greater destiny and a deeper meaning than it possessed at the time of its institution ; they trusted to its spirit leading from one point of light to another and developing higher forces. Just as we cannot obtain a complete knowledge of a tree without regarding not only its root and its stem but also its bark, its branches, and the way in which it blooms, so we cannot form any right estimate of the Christian religion unless we take our stand upon a comprehensive induction that shall cover all the facts of its history. It is true that Christianity has had its classical epoch ; nay more, it had a founder who himself was what he taught—to steep ourselves in him is still the chief matter ; but to restrict ourselves to him means to take a point of view too low for his significance. Individual religious life was what he wanted to kindle and what he did kindle ; it is, as we shall see, his peculiar greatness to have led men to God, so that they may thenceforth live their own life with Him. How, then, can we be silent about the history of the Gospel if we wish to know what he was ?

It may be objected that put in this way the problem is too difficult, and that its solution threatens

to be accompanied by many errors and defects. That
is not to be denied ; but to state a problem in easier
terms, that is to say in this case inaccurately,
because of the difficulties surrounding it, would be a
very perverse expedient. Moreover, even though the
difficulties increase, the work is, on the other hand,
facilitated by the problem being stated in a larger
manner ; for it helps us to grasp what is essential in
the phenomena, and to distinguish kernel and husk.

Jesus Christ and his disciples were situated in
their day just as we are situated in ours ; that is to
say, their feelings, their thoughts, their judgments
and their efforts were bounded by the horizon and
the framework in which their own nation was set
and by its condition at the time. Had it been
otherwise, they would not have been men of flesh
and blood, but spectral beings. For seventeen
hundred years, indeed, people thought, and many
among us still think, that the "humanity" of
Jesus Christ, which is a part of their creed, is sufficiently provided for by the assumption that he had
a human body and a human soul. As if it were
possible to have that without having any definite
character as an individual ! To be a man means,
in the first place, to possess a certain mental and
spiritual disposition, determined in such and such a
way, and thereby limited and circumscribed ; and, in
the second place, it means to be situated, with this
disposition, in an historical environment which in its
turn is also limited and circumscribed. Outside this

there are no such things as "men." It at once
follows, however, that a man can think, speak, and
do absolutely nothing at all in which his peculiar
disposition and his own age are not coefficients. A
single word may seem to be really classical and valid
for all time, and yet the very language in which it is
spoken gives it very palpable limitations. Much less
is a spiritual personality, as a whole, susceptible of
being represented in a way that will banish the
feeling of its limitations, and with those limitations,
the sense of something strange or conventional; and
this feeling must necessarily be enhanced the farther
in point of time the spectator is removed.

From these circumstances it follows that the
historian, whose business and highest duty it is to
determine what is of permanent value, is of necessity required not to cleave to words but to find out
what is essential. The "whole" Christ, the "whole"
Gospel, if we mean by this motto the external image
taken in all its details and set up for imitation, is
just as bad and deceptive a shibboleth as the "whole"
Luther, and the like. It is bad because it enslaves
us, and it is deceptive because the people who proclaim it do not think of taking it seriously, and
could not do so if they tried. They cannot do so
because they cannot cease to feel, understand and
judge as children of their age.

There are only two possibilities here: either the
Gospel is in all respects identical with its earliest
form, in which case it came with its time and has

departed with it; or else it contains something
which, under differing historical forms, is of permanent validity. The latter is the true view. The
history of the Church shows us in its very commencement that "primitive Christianity" had to disappear
in order that "Christianity" might remain; and in
the same way in later ages one metamorphosis
followed upon another. From the beginning it was
a question of getting rid of formulas, correcting
expectations, altering ways of feeling, and this is a
process to which there is no end. But by the very
fact that our survey embraces the whole course as
well as the inception we enhance our standard of
what is essential and of real value.

We enhance our standard, but we need not
wait to take it from the history of those later ages.
The thing itself reveals it. We shall see that the
Gospel in the Gospel is something so simple,
something that speaks to us with so much power,
that it cannot easily be mistaken. No far-reaching
directions as to method, no general introductions, are necessary to enable us to find the way
to it. No one who possesses a fresh eye for
what is alive, and a true feeling for what is really
great, can fail to see it and distinguish it from its
contemporary integument. And even though there
may be many individual aspects of it where the
task of distinguishing what is permanent from what
is fleeting, what is rudimentary from what is
merely historical, is not quite easy, we must not

be like the child who, wanting to get at the kernel
of a bulb, went on picking off the leaves until
there was nothing left, and then could not help seeing that it was just the leaves that made the bulb.
Endeavours of this kind are not unknown in the
history of the Christian religion, but they fade
before those other endeavours which seek to convince us that there is no such thing as either
kernel or husk, growth or decay, but that everything is of equal value and alike permanent.

In these lectures, then, we shall deal first of all
with the Gospel of Jesus Christ, and this theme will
occupy the greater part of our attention. We shall
then show what impression he himself and his Gospel
made upon the first generation of his disciples.
Finally, we shall follow the leading changes which
the Christian idea has undergone in the course of
history, and try to recognise its chief types. What
is common to all the forms which it has taken,
corrected by reference to the Gospel, and, conversely,
the chief features of the Gospel, corrected by reference
to history, will, we may be allowed to hope, bring us
to the kernel of the matter. Within the limits of
a short series of lectures it is, of course, only to what
is important that attention can be called ; but perhaps there will be no disadvantage in fixing our
attention, for once, only on the strong lines and
prominent points of the relief, and, by putting what is
secondary into the background, in looking at the vast
material in a concentrated form. We shall even

refrain, and permissibly refrain, from enlarging, by
way of introduction, on Judaism and its external and
internal relations, and on the Græco-Roman world.
We must never, of course, wholly shut our eyes to
them—nay, we must always keep them in mind; but
diffuse explanations in regard to these matters are
unnecessary.   Jesus Christ's teaching will at once
bring us by steps which, if few, will be great, to
a height where its connexion with Judaism is seen
to be only a loose one, and most of the threads
leading from it into "contemporary history" become
of no importance at all.   This may seem a paradoxical thing to say; for just now we are being
earnestly assured, with an air as though it were some
new discovery that was being imparted to us, that
Jesus Christ's teaching cannot be understood, nay,
cannot be accurately represented, except by having
regard to its connexion with the Jewish doctrines
prevalent at the time, and by first of all setting them
out in full.   There is much that is true in this
statement, and yet, as we shall see, it is incorrect.
It becomes absolutely false, however, when worked
up into the dazzling thesis that the Gospel is intelligible only as the religion of a despairing section
of the Jewish nation; that it was the last effort of
a decadent age, driven by distress into a renunciation
of this earth, and then trying to storm heaven
and demanding civic rights there—a religion of
miserabilism!   It is rather remarkable that the
really desperate were just those who did not welcome

it, but fought against it; remarkable that its leaders, so far as we know them, do not, in fact, bear any of the marks of sickly despair; most remarkable of all, that while indeed renouncing the world and its goods, they establish, in love and holiness, a brotherly union which declares war on the world's misery. The oftener I re-read and consider the Gospels, the more do I find that the contemporary discords, in the midst of which the Gospel stood, and out of which it arose, sink into the background. I entertain no doubt that the founder had his eye upon *man* in whatever external situation he might be found—upon *man* who, fundamentally, always remains the same, whether he be moving upwards or downwards, whether he be in riches or poverty, whether he be of strong mind or of weak. It is the consciousness of all these oppositions being ultimately beneath it, and of its own place above them, that gives the Gospel its sovereignty; for in every man it looks to the point that is unaffected by all these differences. This is very clear in Paul's case; he dominates all earthly things and circumstances like a king, and desires to see them so dominated. The thesis of the decadent age and the religion of the wretched may serve to lead us into the outer court; it may even correctly point to that which originally gave the Gospel its form; but if it is offered us as a key for the understanding of this religion in itself, we must reject it. Moreover, this thesis and the pretensions which it makes are only illustrations of a fashion which has become general in the writing of history, and which in that province will naturally have a longer reign than other fashions, because by its means much that was obscure has, as a matter of fact, been cleared up. But to the heart of the matter its devotees do not penetrate, as they silently assume that no such heart exists.

Let me conclude this lecture by touching briefly on one other important point. In history absolute judgments are impossible. This is a truth which in these days—I say advisedly, in these days—is clear and incontestable. History can only show how things have been; and even where we can throw light upon the past, and understand and criticize it, we must not presume to think that by any process of abstraction absolute judgments as to the value to be assigned to past events can be obtained from the results of a purely historical survey. Such judgments are the creation only of feeling and of will; they are a subjective act. The false notion that the understanding can produce them is a heritage of that protracted epoch in which knowing and knowledge were expected to accomplish everything; in which it was believed that they could be stretched so as to be capable of covering and satisfying all the needs of the mind and the heart. That they cannot do. This is a truth which, in many an hour of ardent work, falls heavily upon our soul, and yet—what a hopeless thing it would be for mankind if the higher peace to which it aspires, and the clearness, the certainty and the strength for which it strives, were dependent on the measure of its learning and its knowledge.

LECTURE II.

OUR first section deals with the main features of the message delivered by Jesus Christ. They include the form in which he delivered what he had to say. We shall see how essential a part of his character is here exhibited, for "he spoke as one having authority and not as the Scribes." But before describing these features I feel it my duty to tell you briefly how matters stand in regard to the sources of our knowledge.

Our authorities for the message which Jesus Christ delivered are—apart from certain important statements made by Paul — the first three Gospels. Everything that we know, independently of these Gospels, about Jesus' history and his teaching, may be easily put on a small sheet of paper, so little does it come to. In particular, the fourth Gospel, which does not emanate or profess to emanate from the apostle John, cannot be taken as an historical authority in the ordinary meaning of the word. The author of it acted with sovereign freedom, transposed events and put them in a strange light, drew up the discourses himself, and illustrated great thoughts

by imaginary situations. Although, therefore, his
work is not altogether devoid of a real, if scarcely re-
cognisable, traditional element, it can hardly make
any claim to be considered an authority for Jesus'
history ; only little of what he says can be accepted,
and that little with caution. On the other hand, it is
an authority of the first rank for answering the question, What vivid views of Jesus' person, what kind
of light and warmth, did the Gospel disengage ?

Sixty years ago David Friedrich Strauss thought
that he had almost entirely destroyed the historical
credibility not only of the fourth but also of the
first three Gospels as well. The historical criticism
of two generations has succeeded in restoring that
credibility in its main outlines. These Gospels are
not, it is true, historical works any more than the
fourth ; they were not written with the simple object
of giving the facts as they were ; they are books
composed for the work of evangelisation. Their
purpose is to awaken a belief in Jesus Christ's
person and mission ; and the purpose is served by
the description of his deeds and discourses, as well
as by the references to the Old Testament. Nevertheless they are not altogether useless as sources of
history, more especially as the object with which
they were written is not supplied from without, but
coincides in part with what Jesus intended. But
such other great leading purposes as have been
ascribed to the evangelists have been one and all
shown to lack any foundation, although with each

individual evangelist many secondary purposes may have come into play. The Gospels are not "party tracts"; neither are they writings which as yet bear the radical impress of the Greek spirit. In their essential substance they belong to the first, the Jewish, epoch of Christianity, that brief epoch which may be denoted as the palæontological. That we possess any reports dating from that time, even though, as is obvious in the first and third Gospel, the setting and the composition are by another hand, is one of those historical arrangements for which we cannot be too thankful. Criticism to-day universally recognises the unique character of the Gospels. What especially marks them off from all subsequent literature is the way in which they state their facts. This species of literary art, which took shape partly by analogy with the didactic narratives of the Jews, and partly from catechetical necessities—this simple and impressive form of exposition was, even a few decades later, no longer capable of exact reproduction. From the time that the Gospel was transferred to the broad ground of the Græco-Roman world it appropriated the literary forms of the Greeks, and the style of the evangelists was then felt to be something strange but sublime. When all is said, the Greek language lies upon these writings only like a diaphanous veil, and it requires hardly any effort to retranslate their contents into Hebrew or Aramaic. That the tradition here presented to us is, in the main, at first hand is obvious.

How fixed this tradition was in regard to its form is proved by the third Gospel. It was composed by a Greek, probably in the time of Domitian; and in the second part of his work, the Acts of the Apostles— besides the preface to the first—he shows us that he was familiar with the literary language of his nation and that he was an excellent master of style. But in the Gospel narrative he did not dare to abandon the traditional type : he tells his story in the same style as Mark and Matthew, with the same connexion of sentences, the same colour, nay, with many of precisely the same details; it is only the ruder words and expressions, which would offend literary taste, that are sparingly corrected.   There is another respect, too, in which his Gospel strikes us as remarkable : he assures us at the beginning of it that he has "had perfect understanding of all things from the very first," and has examined many accounts.   But if we test him by his authorities, we find that he has kept in the main to Mark's Gospel, and to a source which we also find appearing again in Matthew.   These accounts both seemed to him, as a respectable chronicler, to be preferable to the crowd of others.   That offers a good guarantee for them. No historian has found that it is possible or necessary to substitute any other tradition for the one which we have here.

Another point : this tradition is, apart from the story of the Passion, almost exclusively Galilean in its character.   Had not the history of Jesus' public activity been really bounded by this geographical horizon, tradition could not have so described it; for every historical narrative with an eye to effect would have represented him as working chiefly in Jerusalem. That is the account given by the fourth Gospel. That our first three evangelists almost entirely refrain from saying anything about Jerusalem arouses a good prejudice in their favour.

It is true that, measured by the standard of "agreement, inspiration and completeness," these writings leave a very great deal to be desired, and even when judged by a more human standard they suffer from not a few imperfections. Rude additions from a later age they do not, indeed, exhibit—it will always remain a noteworthy fact that, conversely, it is only the fourth Gospel which makes Greeks ask after Jesus —but still they, too, reflect, here and there, the circumstances in which the primitive Christian community was placed and the experiences which it afterwards underwent. People nowadays, however, put such constructions on the text more readily than is necessary. Further, the conviction that Old Testament prophecy was fulfilled in Jesus' history had a disturbing effect on tradition. Lastly, in some of the narratives the miraculous element is obviously intensified. On the other hand, Strauss' contention that the Gospels contain a very great deal that is mythical has not been borne out, even if the very indefinite and defective conception of what "mythical" means in Strauss' application of the word, be allowed to pass. It is almost exclusively in the account of Jesus' childhood, and there only sparingly, that a mythical touch can be traced. None of these disturbing elements affect the heart of the narrative ; not a few of them easily lend themselves to correction, partly by a comparison of the Gospels one with another, partly through the sound judgment that is matured by historical study.

But the miraculous element, all these reports of miracles ! Not Strauss only, but many others too, have allowed themselves to be frightened by them into roundly denying the credibility of the Gospels. But, on the other hand, historical science in this last generation has taken a great step in advance by learning to pass a more intelligent and benevolent judgment on those narratives, and accordingly even reports of the marvellous can now be counted amongst the materials of history and turned to good account. I owe it to you and to the subject briefly to specify the position which historical science to-day takes up in regard to these reports.

In the first place, we know that the Gospels come from a time in which the marvellous may be said to have been something of almost daily occurrence People felt and saw that they were surrounded by wonders, and not by any means only in the religious sphere. Certain spiritualists among us excepted, we are now accustomed to associate the question of miracles exclusively with the question of religion. In those days it was otherwise. The fountains of the marvellous were many. Some sort of divinity was, of course, supposed to be at work in every case; it was a god who accomplished the miracle; but it was not to every god that people stood in a religious relation. Further, in those days, the strict conception which we now attach to the word "miracle" was as yet unknown; it came in only with a knowledge of the laws of nature and their general validity. Before that, no sound insight existed into what was possible and what was impossible, what was rule and what was exception. But where this distinction is not clear, or where, as the case may be, the question has not yet been raised at all in any rigorous form, there are no such things as miracles in the strict sense of the word. No one can feel anything to be an interruption of the order of Nature who does not yet know what the order of Nature is. Miracles, then, could not possess the significance for that age which, if they existed, they would possess for ours. For that age all wonders were only extraordinary events, and, even if they formed a world by themselves, it was certain that there were countless points in which that other world mysteriously encroached upon our own. Nor was it only God's messengers, but magicians and charlatans as well, who were thought to be possessed of some of these miraculous powers. The significance attaching to "miracles" was, therefore, in those days a subject of never-ending controversy; at one moment a high value was set upon them and they were considered to belong to the very essence of religion; at another, they were spoken of with contempt.

In the second place, we now know that it is not after they have been long dead, nor even after the lapse of many years, that miracles have been reported of eminent persons, but at once, often the very next day. The habit of condemning a narrative, or of ascribing it to a later age, only because it includes stories of miracles, is a piece of prejudice.

In the third place, we are firmly convinced that what happens in space and time is subject to the general laws of motion, and that in this sense, as an interruption of the order of Nature, there can be no such things as "miracles." But we also recognise that the religious man—if religion really permeates him and is something more than a belief in the religion of others—is certain that he is not shut up within a blind and brutal course of Nature, but that this course of Nature serves higher ends, or, as it may be, that some inner and divine power can help us so to encounter it as that "everything must necessarily be for the best." This experience, which I might express in one word as the ability to escape from the power and the service of transitory things, is always felt afresh to be a miracle each time that it occurs; it is inseparable from every higher religion, and were it to be surrendered, religion would be at an end. But it is an experience which is equally true of the life of the individual and of the great course of human history. How clearly and logically, then, must a religious man

think, if, in spite of this experience, he holds firmly
to the inviolable character of what happens in
space and time. Who can wonder that even great
minds fail to keep the two spheres quite separate?
And as we all live, first and foremost, in the domain
not of ideas but of perceptions, and in a language
of metaphor, how can we avoid conceiving that
which is divine and makes us free as a mighty
power working upon the order of Nature, and
breaking through or arresting it? This notion,
though it belong only to the realm of fantasy and
metaphor, will, it seems, last as long as religion
itself.

In the fourth place, and lastly, although the order
of Nature be inviolable, we are not yet by any
means acquainted with all the forces working in
it and acting reciprocally with other forces. Our
acquaintance even with the forces inherent in matter,
and with the field of their action, is incomplete;
while of psychic forces we know very much less.
We see that a strong will and a firm faith exert
an influence upon the life of the body, and produce
phenomena which strike us as marvellous. Who
is there up to now that has set any sure bounds
to the province of the possible and the actual?
No one. Who can say how far the influence of
soul upon soul and of soul upon body reaches?
No one. Who can still maintain that any extraordinary phenomenon that may appear in this
domain is entirely based on error and delusion?

Miracles, it is true, do not happen; but of the marvellous and the inexplicable there is plenty. In our present state of knowledge we have become more careful, more hesitating in our judgment, in regard to the stories of the miraculous which we have received from antiquity. That the earth in its course stood still; that a she-ass spoke; that a storm was quieted by a word, we do not believe, and we shall never again believe; but that the lame walked, the blind saw, and the deaf heard, will not be so summarily dismissed as an illusion.

From these suggestions you can arrive for yourselves at the right position to take up in regard to the miraculous stories related in the Gospels, and at their net results. In particular cases, that is to say, in the application of general principles to concrete statements, some uncertainty will always remain. So far as I can judge, the stories may be grouped as follows :—(1) Stories which had their origin in an exaggerated view of natural events of an impressive character; (2) stories which had their origin in sayings or parables, or in the projection of inner experiences on to the external world ; (3) stories such as arose in the interests of the fulfilment of Old Testament sayings; (4) stories of surprising cures effected by Jesus' spiritual force; (5) stories of which we cannot fathom the secret. It is very remarkable, however, that Jesus himself did not assign that critical importance to his

miraculous deeds which even the evangelist Mark
and the others all attributed to them. Did he not
exclaim, in tones of complaint and accusation, " Unless
ye see signs and wonders, ye will not believe"? He
who uttered these words cannot have held that
belief in the wonders which he wrought was the
right or the only avenue to the recognition of his
person and his mission; nay, in all essential points
he must have thought of them quite otherwise than
his evangelists. And the remarkable fact that these
very evangelists, without appreciating its range,
hand down the statement that Jesus "did not many
mighty works there because of their unbelief," shows
us, from another and a different side, with what
caution we must receive these miraculous stories,
and into what category we must put them.

It follows from all this that we must not try to
evade the Gospel by entrenching ourselves behind
the miraculous stories related by the evangelists.
In spite of those stories, nay, in part even in
them, we are presented with a reality which has
claims upon our participation. Study it, and do not
let yourselves be deterred because this or that
miraculous story strikes you as strange or leaves
you cold. If there is anything here that you find
unintelligible, put it quietly aside. Perhaps you
will have to leave it there for ever; perhaps the
meaning will dawn upon you later and the story
assume a significance of which you never dreamt.
Once more, let me say : do not be deterred. The

question of miracles is of relative indifference in comparison with everything else which is to be found in the Gospels. It is not miracles that matter; the question on which everything turns is whether we are helplessly yoked to an inexorable necessity, or whether a God exists who rules and governs, and whose power to compel Nature we can move by prayer and make a part of our experience.

Our evangelists, as we know, do not tell us anything about the history of Jesus' early development; they tell us only of his public activity. Two of the Gospels do, it is true, contain an introductory history (the history of Jesus' birth); but we may disregard it; for even if it contained something more trustworthy than it does actually contain, it would be as good as useless for our purpose. That is to say, the evangelists themselves never refer to it, nor make Jesus himself refer to his antecedents. On the contrary, they tell us that Jesus' mother and his brethren were completely surprised at his coming forward, and did not know what to make of it. Paul, too, is silent; so that we can be sure that the oldest tradition knew nothing of any stories of Jesus' birth.

We know nothing of Jesus' history for the first thirty years of his life. Is there not a terrible uncertainty here? What is there left us if we have to begin our task by confessing that we are unable to write any life of Jesus? How can we write the history of a man of whose development we know

nothing, and with only a year or two of whose life
we are acquainted ? Now, however certain it may be
that our materials are insufficient for a " biography,"
they are very weighty in other respects, and even
their silence on the first thirty years is instructive.
They are weighty because they give us information
upon three important points : *In the first place, they
offer us a plain picture of Jesus' teaching, in
regard both to its main features and to its individual application; in the second place, they tell
us how his life issued in the service of his vocation;
and in the third place, they describe to us the
impression which he made upon his disciples, and
which they transmitted.*

These are, in fact, three important points ; nay,
they are the points on which everything turns. It
is because we can get a clear view of them that a
characteristic picture of Jesus is possible; or, to
speak more modestly, that there is some hope for
an attempt to understand what his aims were, what
he was, and what he signifies for us.

As regards the thirty years of silence, we gather
from our evangelists that Jesus did not think it
necessary to give his disciples any information about
them. But much may be said about them negatively. First of all, it is very improbable that he
went through any Rabbinical school ; he nowhere
speaks like a man who had assimilated any theological culture of a technical kind, or learned the art
of scholarly exegesis. Compare him in this respect

with the apostle Paul; how clearly it can be seen from the latter's epistles that he had sat at the feet of theological teachers. With Jesus we find nothing of the kind; and hence he caused a stir by appearing in the schools and teaching at all. He lived and had his being in the sacred writings, but not after the manner of a professional teacher.

Neither can he have had any relations with the Essenes, a remarkable order of Jewish monks. Were that so, he would have belonged to the pupils who show their dependence on their teachers by proclaiming and doing the opposite of what they have been taught. The Essenes made a point of the most extreme purity in the eye of the law, and held severely aloof not only from the impure but even from those who were a little lax in their purity. It is only thus that we can understand their living strictly apart, their dwelling in particular places, and their practice of frequent ablutions every day. Jesus exhibits a complete contrast with this mode of life : he goes in search of sinners and eats with them. So fundamental a difference alone makes it certain that he had nothing to do with the Essenes. His aims and the means which he employed divide him off from them. If he appears to coincide with them in many of his individual injunctions to his disciples, these are accidental points of contact, as his motives were quite other than theirs.

Further, unless all appearances are deceptive, no stormy crisis, no breach with his past, lies behind

the period of Jesus' life that we know. In none of
his sayings or discourses, whether he is threatening
and punishing or drawing and calling people to him
with kindness, whether he is speaking of his relation
to the Father or to the world, can we discover the
signs of inner revolutions overcome, or the scars of
any terrible conflict. Everything seems to pour from
him naturally, as though it could not do otherwise,
like a spring from the depths of the earth, clear and
unchecked in its flow. Where shall we find the man
who at the age of thirty can so speak, if he has gone
through bitter struggles—struggles of the soul, in
which he has ended by burning what he once
adored, and by adoring what he burned? Where
shall we find the man who has broken with his past,
in order to summon others to repentance as well as
himself, but who through it all never speaks of
his own repentance? This consideration makes it
impossible that his life could have been spent in inner
conflict, however little it may have been lacking in
deep emotion, in temptation and in doubt.

One final point: the picture of Jesus' life and his
discourses stand in no relation with the Greek spirit.
That is almost a matter for surprise ; for Galilee was
full of Greeks, and Greek was then spoken in many
of its cities, much as Swedish is nowadays in Finland.
There were Greek teachers and philosophers there,
and it is scarcely conceivable that Jesus should have
been entirely unacquainted with their language. But
that he was in any way influenced by them, that he

was ever in touch with the thoughts of Plato or
the Porch, even though it may have been only in
some popular redaction, it is absolutely impossible to
maintain. Of course if religious individualism—God
and the soul, the soul and its God ; if subjectivism ;
if the full self-responsibility of the individual ; if the
separation of the religious from the political—if all
this is only Greek, then Jesus, too, stands within the
sphere of Greek development ; then he, too, breathed
the pure air of Greece and drank from the Greek
spring. But it cannot be proved that it is only on
this one line, only in the Hellenic people, that this
development took place ; nay, it is rather the contrary that can be shown ; other nations also advanced
to similar states of knowledge and feeling ; although
they did so, it is true, as a rule, only after Alexander
the Great had pulled down the barriers and fences
which separated the peoples. For these nations, too,
no doubt it was in the majority of cases the Greek
element that was the liberating and progressive factor.
But I do not believe that the Psalmist who uttered
the words, " Whom have I in heaven but thee ? and
there is none upon earth that I desire beside thee,"
had ever heard anything of Socrates or of Plato.

Enough : from their silence on the first thirty
years of Jesus' life, and from what the evangelists do
not tell us of the period of his activity, there are
important things to be learnt.

He lived in religion, and it was breath to him in

the fear of God; his whole life, all his thoughts and feelings, were absorbed in the relation to God, and yet he did not talk like an enthusiast and a fanatic, who sees only one red-hot spot, and so is blind to the world and all that it contains. He spoke his message and looked at the world with a fresh and clear eye for the life, great and small, that surrounded him. He proclaimed that to gain the whole world was nothing if the soul were injured, and yet he remained kind and sympathetic to every living thing. That is the most astonishing and the greatest fact about him! His discourses, generally in the form of parables and sayings, exhibit every degree of human speech and the whole range of the emotions. The sternest tones of passionate accusation and indignant reproof, nay, even irony, he does not despise; but they must have formed the exception with him. He is possessed of a quiet, uniform, collected demeanour, with everything directed to one goal. He never uses any ecstatic language, and the tone of stirring prophecy is rare. Entrusted with the greatest of all missions, his eye and ear are open to every impression of the life around him—a proof of intense calm and absolute certainty. "Mourning and weeping, laughing and dancing, wealth and poverty, hunger and thirst, health and sickness, children's play and politics, gathering and scattering, the leaving of home, life in the inn and the return, marriage and funeral, the splendid house of the living and the grave of the

dead, the sower and the reaper in the field, the lord
of the vintage among his vines, the idle workman
in the marketplace, the shepherd searching for the
sheep, the dealer in pearls on the sea, and, then
again, the woman at home anxious over the barrel
of meal and the leaven, or the lost piece of money,
the widow's complaint to the surly official, the
earthly food that perishes, the mental relation of
teacher and pupil, on the one side regal glory and
the tyrant's lust of power, on the other childish
innocence and the industry of the servant—all these
pictures enliven his discourse and make it clear
even to those who are children in mind." They do
more than tell us that he spoke in picture and
parable. They exhibit an inner freedom and a
cheerfulness of soul in the midst of the greatest
strain, such as no prophet ever possessed before
him. His eye rests kindly upon the flowers and
the children, on the lily of the field—"Solomon in all
his glory is not clothed like one of them"—on the
birds in the air and the sparrows on the house-top.
The sphere in which he lived, above the earth and
its concerns, did not destroy his interest in it; no!
he brought everything in it into relation with
the God whom he knew, and he saw it as protected
in him : " Your Father in heaven feeds them." The
parable is his most familiar form of speech. Insensibly, however, parable and sympathy pass into
each other. Yet he who had not where to lay his
head does not speak like one who has broken with

everything, or like an heroic penitent, or like an ecstatic prophet, but like a man who has rest and peace for his soul, and is able to give life and strength to others. He strikes the mightiest notes; he offers men an inexorable alternative; he leaves them no escape; and yet the strongest emotion seems to come naturally to him, and he expresses it as something natural; he clothes it in the language in which a mother speaks to her child.

LECTURE III.

In the previous lecture we spoke of our evangelists and of their silence on the subject of Jesus' early development. We described in brief the mode and character of his teaching. We saw that he spoke like a prophet and yet not like a prophet. His words breathe peace, joy, and certainty. He urges the necessity of struggle and decision—"where your treasure is, there will your heart be also"—and yet the quiet symmetry of a parable is over all that he says: under God's sun and the dew of heaven everything is to grow and increase until the harvest. He lived in the continual consciousness of God's presence. His food and drink was to do God's will. But—and this seemed to us the greatest thing about him and the seal of his inner freedom—he did not speak like an heroic penitent, or like an ascetic who has turned his back upon the world. His eye rested kindly upon the whole world, and he saw it as it was, in all its varied and changing colours. He ennobled it in his parables; his gaze penetrated the veil of the earthly, and he recognised everywhere the hand of the living God.

When he came forward, another was already at work among the Jewish people : John the Baptist. Within a few months a great movement had arisen on the banks of the Jordan. It differed altogether from those messianic movements which for several generations had by fits and starts kept the nation alive. The Baptist, it is true, also proclaimed that the kingdom of God was at hand ; and that meant nothing less than that the day of the Lord, the judgment, the end, was then coming. But the day of judgment which John the Baptist announced was not the day when God was going to take vengeance upon the heathen and raise up his own people ; it was the day of judgment for this very people that he prophesied. " Who hath warned you to flee from the wrath to come ? Think not to say within yourselves, We have Abraham to our father : for I say unto you that God is able of these stones to raise up children unto Abraham. And now also the axe is laid unto the root of the trees." In that day of judgment it is not being children of Abraham, but doing works of righteousness, which is to turn the scale. And he, the preacher, himself began with repentance and devoted his life to it ; he stands before them in raiment of camel's hair, and his meat is locusts and wild honey. But it is not in the levying of a band of ascetics that he sees his work, or at any rate his main work. He appeals to the whole nation, busy with its various trades and callings, and summons it to repentance. They seem

very simple truths that he utters : to the publicans
he says : "Exact no more than that which is
appointed you"; to the soldiers: "Do violence
to no man, neither accuse any falsely, and be
content with your wages"; to the well-to-do:
"He that hath two coats, let him impart to him
that hath none, and he that hath meat, let him
do likewise"; and to all: "Forget not the poor."
This is the practical proof of the repentance to which
he calls, and it embraces the conversion which he
has in view. It is not a question of a single act,
the baptism of repentance, but of a righteous life in
the face of the avenging justice of God. Of ceremonies, sacrifices, and the works of the law, John
did not speak; apparently he thought them un-
important. It was on a right disposition and good
deeds that everything turned. In the day of
judgment it was by this standard that the God of
Abraham would judge.

Let us pause here for a moment. Questions force
themselves upon us at this point which have often
been answered and still are again and again put.
It is clear that John the Baptist proclaimed the
sovereignty of God and his holy moral law. It is
also clear that he proclaimed to his fellow-country-
men that it was by the moral law that they were to
measure, and that on this alone everything was to
turn. He told them that what they were to care
about most was to be in a right state within and
to do good deeds. It is clear, lastly, that there is

nothing over-refined or artificial in his notion of what
was good; he means ordinary morality. It is here
that the questions arise.

Firstly : if it was only so simple a matter as the
eternal claims of what is right and holy, why all this
apparatus about the coming of the day of judgment,
about the axe being laid to the root of the trees,
about the unquenchable fire, and so on ?

Secondly : is not this baptism in the wilderness
and this proclamation that the day of judgment was
at hand simply the reflection or the product of the
political and social state of the nation at the time ?

Thirdly : what is there that is really new in this
proclamation and had not been already expressed in
Judaism ?

These three questions are very intimately connected with one another.

Firstly, then, as to the whole dramatic eschatological
apparatus about the coming of the kingdom of God,
the end being at hand, and so on. Well, every time
that a man earnestly, and out of the depths of his
own personal experience, points others to God and to
what is good and holy, whether it be deliverance or
judgment that he preaches, it has always, so far as
history tells us, taken the form of announcing that
the end is at hand. How is that to be explained ?
The answer is not difficult. Not only is religion a
life in and with God; but, just because it is that, it
is also the revelation of the meaning and responsibility of life. Every one who has awakened to a

sense of religion perceives that, without it, the search
for such meaning is in vain, and that the individual,
as well as the multitude, wanders aimlessly and falls :
" they go astray ; every one turns to his own way."
But the prophet who has become conscious of God is
filled with terror and agony as he recognises that all
mankind is sunk in error and indifference. He feels
like a traveller who sees his companions blindly
rushing to the edge of a precipice. He wants to call
them back at all costs. The time is running out ; he
can still warn them ; he can still adjure them to turn
back ; in a single hour, perhaps, all will be lost. The
time is running out, it is the last moment—this is
the cry in which, then, in all nations and at all
times, any energetic call to conversion has been
voiced whenever a fresh prophet has been granted
them. The prophet's gaze penetrates the course of
history ; he sees the irrevocable end ; and he is filled
with boundless astonishment that the godlessness and
blindness, the frivolity and indolence, have not long
since brought everything to utter ruin and destruction. That there is still a brief moment left in which
conversion is possible seems to him the greatest
marvel of all, and to be ascribed only to God's
forbearance. But certain it is that the end cannot
be very far off. This is the way in which with every
great cry for repentance the idea of the approaching
end always arises. The individual forms in which it
shapes itself depend upon contemporary circumstances
and are of subordinate importance. It is only the

religion which has been built up into an intellectual
system that does not make this emphasising of the
end all-important; without such emphasis no actual
religion is conceivable, whether it springs up anew like
a sudden flame or glows in the soul like a secret fire.

I pass now to the second question : whether the
social and political conditions of the time were not
causes of the religious movement. Let us see briefly
where we are. You are aware that at the time of
which we speak the peaceful days of the Jewish
theocracy were long past. For two centuries blow
had followed upon blow ; from the terrible days of
Antiochus Epiphanes onwards the nation had never
had any rest. The kingdom of the Maccabees had
been set up, and through inner strife and external
foe had soon disappeared again. The Romans had
invaded the country and had laid their iron hand
upon everything. The tyranny of that Edomite par-
venu, King Herod, had robbed the nation of every
pleasure in life and maimed it in all its members.
So far as human foresight went, it looked as if no
improvement in its position could ever again be
effected ; the lie seemed to be given to all the
glorious old prophecies ; the end appeared to have
come. How easy it was at such an epoch to despair
of all earthly things, and in this despair to renounce
in utter distress what had once passed as the inseparable accompaniment of the theocracy. How
easy it was now to declare the earthly crown,
political possessions, prestige and wealth, strenuous

effort and struggle, to be one and all worthless, and in place of them to look to heaven for a completely new kingdom, a kingdom for the poor, the oppressed, the weak, and to hope that their virtues of gentleness and patience would receive a crown. And if for hundreds of years the national God of Israel had been undergoing a transformation; if he had broken in pieces the weapons of the mighty, and derided the showy worship of his priests; if he had demanded righteous judgment and mercy— what a temptation there was to proclaim him as the God who wills to see his people in misery that he may then bring them deliverance! We can, in fact, with a few touches construct the religion and its hopes which seemed of necessity to result from the circumstances of the time — a miserabilism which clings to the expectation of a miraculous interference on God's part, and in the meantime, as it were, wallows in wretchedness.

But although the terrible circumstances of the time certainly disengaged and developed many ideas of this kind, and easily account for the wild enterprises of the false Messiahs and the political efforts of fanatical Pharisees, they are very far from being sufficient to explain John the Baptist's message. They do, indeed, explain how it was that deliverance from earthly things was an idea which seized hold of wide circles, and that people were looking to God. Trouble makes men pray. But trouble in itself does not give any moral force, and moral force was the chief element in John the Baptist's message. In appealing to it, in proclaiming that everything must be based on morality and personal responsibility, he took a higher point of view than the feeble piety of the "poor," and drew not from time but from eternity.

It is scarcely a century since Fichte delivered his memorable orations here in Berlin, after the terrible defeat which Germany had suffered. What did he do in these lectures? In the first place, he held up a mirror to the nation, and showed it its sins and their consequences,—frivolity, godlessness, self-complacency, infatuation, weakness. What did he do next? Did he simply call them to arms? Arms were just what they were no longer capable of bearing; they had been struck from their powerless hands. It was to repentance and to inward conversion that he called them; to God, and therefore to the exertion of all their moral force; to truth and to the Spirit, so that by the Spirit everything might be made new. By his powerful personality, and in union with friends of a like mind, he produced an immense impression. He succeeded in opening up once more the choked fountains of our energy, because he knew the strength from which help comes and had drunk of the living water himself. No doubt the necessities of the time taught him and steeled him; but it would be foolish and ridiculous to maintain that Fichte's orations were the product of the general woe. They are the

antithesis of it. Not otherwise must we think of
John the Baptist's message, and—let me say it at
once—of the message which Jesus himself delivered.
That they appealed to those who expected nothing
of the world or of politics—of John the Baptist,
however, this is not directly reported; that they
would have nothing to do with those popular
leaders who had led the people to ruin; that they
turned their gaze altogether from earthly things, may
also be accounted for by the circumstances of the
time. But the remedy which they proclaimed was
no product of those circumstances. Nay, was not
calling people to ordinary morality and expecting
everything of it bound to seem a hopeless enterprise? And whence came the power, the inflexible
power, which compelled others? This leads us to
the last of the questions which we have raised.

Thirdly, what was there that was new in the
whole movement? Was it anything new to set up
the sovereignty of God, the sovereignty of the good
and the holy, in opposition to all the other elements
which had forced their way into religion? Did
John the Baptist, did Christ himself, bring in anything that had not been proclaimed long before?
Gentlemen, the question as to what is new in
religion is not a question which is raised by those
who live in it. What is there that can have been
" new," seeing that mankind existed so long before
Jesus Christ and had seen so much in the way of
intelligence and knowledge? Monotheism had long

been introduced, and the few possible types of monotheistic religious fervour had long made their appearance here and there, and had taken possession of whole schools, nay, of a whole nation. Can the religious individualism of that Psalmist ever be surpassed in depth and vigour who confessed: " Lord, when I have thee, I ask not after heaven and earth "? Can we go beyond what Micah said: " He hath showed thee, O man, what is good; and what doth the Lord require of thee but to do justly and to love mercy, and to walk humbly with thy God "? Centuries had passed since these words were spoken. " What do you want with your Christ," we are asked, principally by Jewish scholars; " he introduced nothing new." I answer with Wellhausen: It is quite true that what Jesus proclaimed, what John the Baptist expressed before him in his exhortations to repentance, was also to be found in the prophets, and even in the Jewish tradition of their time. The Pharisees themselves were in possession of it; but unfortunately they were in possession of much else besides. With them it was weighted, darkened, distorted, rendered ineffective and deprived of its force, by a thousand things which they also held to be religious and every whit as important as mercy and judgment. They reduced everything to one dead level, wove everything into one fabric; the good and holy was only one woof in a broad earthly warp. You ask again, then: " What was there that was new?" The question is out of place in

monotheistic religion. Ask rather : " Had what
was here proclaimed any strength and any vigour ? "
I answer : Take the people of Israel and search
the whole history of their religion ; take history
generally, and where will you find any message about
God and the good that was ever so pure and so full
of strength—for purity and strength go together—
as we hear and read of in the Gospels ? As regards
purity, the spring of holiness had, indeed, long been
opened ; but it was choked with sand and dirt, and
its water was polluted. For rabbis and theologians
to come afterwards and distil this water, even if
they were successful, makes no difference. But
now the spring burst forth afresh, and broke
a new way for itself through the rubbish —
through the rubbish which priests and theologians
had heaped up so as to smother the true element
in religion ; for how often does it happen in history
that theology is only the instrument by which
religion is discarded ! The other element was that
of strength. Pharisaical teachers had proclaimed
that everything was contained in the injunction to
love God and one's neighbour. They spoke excellently ; the words might have come out of Jesus'
mouth. But what was the result of their language ?
That the nation, that in particular their own pupils,
condemned the man who took the words seriously.
All that they did was weak and, because weak,
harmful. Words effect nothing ; it is the power
of the personality that stands behind them. But he

" taught as one having authority and not as the Scribes." Such was the impression of him which his disciples received. His words became to them " the words of life," seeds which sprang up and bore fruit. That was what was new.

Some such message John the Baptist had already begun to deliver. He, too, had undoubtedly placed himself in opposition to the leaders of the people ; for any man who tells people to " reform," and at the same time enjoins nothing more than repentance and good works, always comes into opposition with the official leaders of religion and church. But beyond the lines of the message of repentance John did not go.

Jesus Christ then appeared. He first of all accepted and affirmed the Baptist's message to its full extent, and he acknowledged the Baptist himself ; nay, there was no one of whom he spoke in language of such warm recognition. Did not he say that among them that were born of women there had not arisen a greater than John the Baptist ? Again and again he acknowledged that his cause began with the Baptist and that he was his forerunner. Nay, he had himself been baptised by him, and thereby put himself into the movement which the Baptist began.

But he did not rest there. When he appeared, he, too, it is true, like John proclaimed : " Repent, for the kingdom of God is at hand " ; but his message became one of joy as he delivered it. The traditions about him contain nothing more certain than that his message was an " evangel," and that it was felt to bring blessing and joy. With good reason, therefore, the evangelist Luke began his narrative of Jesus' public appearance with the words of the prophet Isaiah :—" *The Spirit of the Lord is upon me, because he hath anointed me to preach the gospel to the poor; he hath sent me to heal the broken-hearted, to preach deliverance to the captives and recovering of sight to the blind, to set at liberty them that are bruised, to preach the acceptable year of the Lord.*" Or in Jesus' own words :—" *Come unto me all ye that labour and are heavy laden and I will give you rest. Take my yoke upon you, and learn of me; for I am meek and lowly of heart; and ye shall find rest unto your souls. For my yoke is easy and my burden is light.*" These words dominated Jesus' whole work and message; they contain the theme of all that he taught and did. They make it at once obvious that in this teaching of his he left John the Baptist's message far behind. The latter, although already in silent conflict with the priests and the scribes, did not become a definite signal for contradiction. " The falling and the rising again," a new humanity opposed to the old, the God-man—Jesus Christ—was the first to create. He came into immediate opposition with the official leaders of the people, and in them with ordinary human nature in general. They thought of God as of a despot guarding the ceremonial observances in His household; he breathed in the presence of God. They saw Him only in His law, which they had converted into a labyrinth of dark defiles, blind alleys and secret passages; he saw and felt Him everywhere. They were in possession of a thousand of His commandments, and thought, therefore, that they knew Him; he had one only, and knew Him by it. They had made this religion into an earthly trade, and there was nothing more detestable; he proclaimed the living God and the soul's nobility.

If, however, we take a general view of Jesus' teaching, we shall see that it may be grouped under three heads. They are each of such a nature as to contain the whole, and hence it can be exhibited in its entirety under any one of them.

Firstly, the kingdom of God and its coming.

Secondly, God the Father and the infinite value of the human soul.

Thirdly, the higher righteousness and the commandment of love.

That Jesus' message is so great and so powerful lies in the fact that it is so simple and on the other hand so rich; so simple as to be exhausted in each of the leading thoughts which he uttered; so rich that every one of these thoughts seems to be inexhaustible and the full meaning of the sayings and parables beyond our reach. But more than that—he himself stands behind everything that he said. His words speak to us across the centuries with the freshness of the present. It is here that that profound saying is truly verified: " Speak, that I may see thee."

Our course in what follows will be to try to learn
what those three heads are, and to classify the
thoughts which come under them. They contain the
main features of Jesus' message. We shall then try
to understand the Gospel in its relations to certain
great questions of life.

I. *The kingdom of God and its coming.*

Jesus' message of the kingdom of God runs through
all the forms and statements of the prophecy which,
taking its colour from the Old Testament, announces
the day of judgment and the visible government of
God in the future, up to the idea of an inward coming
of the kingdom, starting with Jesus' message and then
beginning. His message embraces these two poles,
with many stages between them that shade off one
into another. At the one pole the coming of the
kingdom seems to be a purely future event, and the
kingdom itself to be the external rule of God ; at the
other, it appears as something inward, something
which is already present and making its entrance at
the moment. You see, therefore, that neither the conception of the kingdom of God, nor the way in which
its coming is represented, is free from ambiguity.
Jesus took it from the religious traditions of his
nation, where it already occupied a foremost place ;
he accepted various aspects of it in which the conception was still a living force, and he added new ones.

Eudemonistic expectations of a mundane and political character were all that he discarded.

Jesus, like all those of his own nation who were really in earnest, was profoundly conscious of the great antithesis between the kingdom of God and that kingdom of the world in which he saw the reign of evil and the evil one. This was no mere image or empty idea; it was a truth which he saw and felt most vividly. He was certain, then, that the kingdom of the world must perish and be destroyed. But nothing short of a battle can effect it. With dramatic intensity battle and victory stand like a picture before his soul, drawn in those large firm lines in which the prophets had seen them. At the close of the drama he sees himself seated at the right hand of his Father, and his twelve disciples on thrones judging the twelve tribes of Israel; so objective was this picture to him, so completely in harmony with the ideas of his time. Now we may take the view—and not a few of us take it—that in these dramatic pictures, with their hard colours and contrasts, we have the actual purport of Jesus' message and the fundamental form which it took; and that all his other statements of it must be simply regarded as secondary. We may say that they are all variations of it more or less edifying, variations which were added, perhaps, only by later reporters; but that the only positive factor is the dramatic hope for the future. In this view I cannot concur. It is considered a perverse procedure in similar cases to judge eminent, epoch-making per-

sonalities first and foremost by what they share with
their contemporaries, and on the other hand to put
what is great and characteristic in them into the
background.   The tendency as far as possible to
reduce everything to one level, and to efface what
is special and individual, may spring in some minds
from a praiseworthy sense of truth, but it has proved
misleading.   More frequently, however, we get the
endeavour, conscious or unconscious, to refuse greatness any recognition at all, and to throw down anything that is exalted.   There can be no doubt about
the fact that the idea of the two kingdoms, of God
and of the devil, and their conflicts, and of that last
conflict at some future time when the devil, long
since cast out of heaven, will be also defeated on
earth, was an idea which Jesus simply shared with
his contemporaries.   He did not start it, but he grew
up in it and he retained it.   The other view, however, that the kingdom of God "cometh not with
observation," that it is already here, was his own.

For us, gentlemen, to-day, it is difficult to reconcile,
nay, it is scarcely possible to bridge over, such an
opposition as is involved, on the one side in a
dramatic picture of God's kingdom existing in the
future, and on the other in the announcement that
"it is in the midst of you," a still and mighty power
in the hearts of men.   But to understand why it was
that with other historical traditions and other forms
of culture no opposition was felt to exist between
these views, nay, that both were able to exist side

by side, we must reflect, we must steep ourselves in the history of the past. I imagine that a few hundred years hence there will be found to exist in the intellectual ideas which we shall have left behind us much that is contradictory ; people will wonder how we put up with it. They will find much hard and dry husk in what we took for the kernel ; they will be unable to understand how we could be so short-sighted, and fail to get a sound grasp of what was essential and separate it from the rest. Some day the knife will be applied and pieces will be cut away where as yet we do not feel the slightest inclination to distinguish. Let us hope that then we may find fair judges, who will measure our ideas not by what we have unwittingly taken over from tradition and are neither able nor called upon to correct, but by what was born of our very own, by the changes and improvements which we have effected in what was handed down to us or was commonly prevalent in our day.

Truly the historian's task of distinguishing between what is traditional and what is peculiar, between kernel and husk, in Jesus' message of the kingdom of God is a difficult and responsible one. How far may we go ? We do not want to rob this message of its innate character and colour, we do not want to change it into a pale scheme of ethics. On the other hand, we do not want to lose sight of its peculiar character and strength, as we should do were we to side with those who resolve it into the general ideas

prevailing at the time. The very way in which
Jesus distinguished between the traditional elements
—he left out none in which there was a spark of
moral force, and he accepted none which encouraged
the selfish expectations of his nation—this very
discrimination teaches us that it was from a deeper
knowledge that he spoke and taught. But we possess
testimonies of a much more striking kind. If anyone
wants to know what the kingdom of God and the
coming of it meant in Jesus' message, he must read
and study his parables. He will then see what it
is that is meant. The kingdom of God comes by
coming to the individual, by entering into his soul
and laying hold of it. True, the kingdom of God is
the rule of God; but it is the rule of the holy God in
the hearts of individuals; *it is God himself in his
power*. From this point of view everything that
is dramatic in the external and historical sense has
vanished; and gone, too, are all the external hopes
for the future. Take whatever parable you will, the
parable of the sower, of the pearl of great price, of
the treasure buried in the field—the word of God,
God himself, is the kingdom. It is not a question of
angels and devils, thrones and principalities, but of
God and the soul, the soul and its God.

LECTURE IV.

We last spoke of Jesus' message in so far as it proclaimed the kingdom of God and its coming. We saw that it runs through all the forms in which the prophecy of the day of judgment is expressed in the Old Testament, up to the idea of an inward coming of the kingdom then beginning. Finally we tried to show why the latter idea is to be regarded as the dominant one. Before examining it more closely, however, I should like to draw your attention to two particularly important expressions of it, lying between the extremes of the "day of judgment" and the "inner coming."

In the first of them, the coming of the kingdom of God signifies that the kingdom of the devil is destroyed and the demons vanquished. Hitherto it is they who have been ruling; they have taken possession of men and even of whole nations, and forced them to their will. Jesus not only declares that he is come to destroy the works of the devil, but he actually drives out the demons and releases men from their power.

Let me here digress a little from our subject.

Nothing in the Gospels strikes us as stranger than
the frequently recurring stories of demons, and the
great importance which the evangelists attach to
them. For many among us the very fact that these
writings report such absurdities is sufficient reason
for declining to accept them. Now in this connexion
it is well to know that absolutely similar stories are
to be found in numerous writings of that age, Greek,
Roman, and Jewish. The notion of people being
" possessed " was current everywhere ; nay, even the
science of the time looked upon a whole section of
morbid phenomena in this light. But the consequence of these phenomena being explained as
meaning that some evil and invisible power had taken
possession of a man was that mental affections took
forms which looked as if an alien being had really
entered into the soul. There is nothing paradoxical
in this. If modern science were to declare nervous
disease to consist, in great part, of " possession," and
the newspapers were to spread this announcement
amongst the public, the same thing would recur. We
should soon have numerous cases in which nervous
patients looked as if they were in the grip of an evil
spirit and themselves believed that they were so.
Theory and belief would work by suggestion and
again create a class of " demoniacs " amongst the
insane, just as they created them hundreds, nay
thousands, of years ago. It is unhistorical and
foolish to attribute any peculiar notion or " theory "
about demons and the demoniac to the Gospels and

the evangelists. They only shared the general notions of their time. The forms of mental disease in question are of rare occurrence nowadays, but nevertheless they are not yet quite extinct. Where they occur the best means of encountering them is to-day, as it was formerly, the influence of a strong personality. It manages to threaten and subdue the "devil" and so heal the patient. In Palestine " demoniacs " must have been particularly numerous. Jesus saw in them the forces of evil and mischief, and by his marvellous power over the souls of those who trusted him he banished the disease. This brings us to the second point.

When John the Baptist in prison was disturbed by doubts as to whether Jesus was " he who was to come," he sent two of his own disciples to him to ask him himself. There is nothing more touching than this question of the Baptist's, nothing more edifying than the Lord's answer. But we will not dwell upon the scene. What was the answer? " Go and shew John again those things which you do hear and see : the blind receive their sight, and the lame walk, the lepers are cleansed, and the deaf hear, the dead are raised up, and the poor have the Gospel preached to them." That is what the " coming of the kingdom " means, or, rather, it is there already in this saving activity. By vanquishing and banishing misery, need and disease, by the actual influence which Jesus was exerting, John was to see that a new day had dawned. The healing of the possessed was only

a part of this saving activity; the activity itself,
however, was what Jesus denoted as the meaning
and the seal of his mission. It was, then, to the
wretched, to the sick, and to the poor, that he
addressed himself; but not as a moralist and without any trace of weak-minded sentimentality. He
makes no division of evils into departments and
groups; he spends no time in asking whether the
sick one "deserves" to be healed; he is far, too,
from having any sympathy for pain and death. He
nowhere says that disease is salutary and that evil
is a blessing. No! disease he calls disease, and
health he calls health. To him all evil, all misery,
is something terrible; it is part of the great realm
of Satan. But he feels the power of the Saviour
within him. He knows that progress is possible
only by overcoming weakness and healing disease.

But he goes further. It is by his healing, above
all by his forgiving sin, that the kingdom of God
comes. This is the first complete transition to
the conception of the kingdom of God as the power
that works inwardly. As he calls the sick and the
poor to him, so he calls sinners also, and it is this
call which is all-important. "The Son of Man
is come to seek and to save that which was lost."
Here for the first time everything that is external
and merely future is abandoned : it is the individual,
not the nation or the state, which is redeemed ; it
is new men who are to arise, and the kingdom of
God is to be at once their strength and the goal

at which they aim. They search for the treasure hidden in the field and find it; they sell all that they have and buy the pearl of great price; they are converted and become as children; but thereby they are redeemed and made God's children and God's champions.

It was in this connexion that Jesus spoke of the kingdom of God which the violent take by force, and, again, of the kingdom of God which grows steadily and silently like a seed and bears fruit. It is in the nature of spiritual force, a power which sinks into a man within, and can be understood only from within. Thus, although the kingdom is also in heaven; although it will come with the day of judgment, he can still say of it: "It is not here or there, it is within you."

At a later period the view of the kingdom, according to which it was already come and still comes in Jesus' saving activity, was not kept up by his disciples: nay, they continued to speak of it as of something that was solely in the future. But the thing itself retained its force; it was only given another title. It underwent the same experience as the conception of the "Messiah." As we shall see hereafter, there was scarcely anyone in the Church of the Gentiles who sought to explain Jesus' significance by regarding him as the "Messiah." But the thing itself did not perish.

The essential elements in the message of the kingdom were preserved. The kingdom has a triple meaning.

Firstly, it is something supernatural, a gift from above, not a product of ordinary life. Secondly, it is a purely religious blessing, the inner link with the living God; thirdly, it is the most important experience that a man can have, that on which everything else depends; it permeates and dominates his whole existence, because sin is forgiven and misery banished.

This kingdom, which comes to the humble and makes them new men and joyful, is the key that first unlocks the meaning and the aim of life. This was what Jesus himself found, and what his disciples found. It is a supernatural element alone that ever enables us to get at the meaning of life; for natural existence ends in death. But a life that is bound up with death can have no meaning; it is only sophisms that can blind us to this fact. But here the kingdom of God, the Eternal, entered into time. "Eternal light came in and made the world look new." This is Jesus' message of the kingdom. Everything else that he proclaimed can be brought into connexion with this; his whole " doctrine " can be conceived as a message of the kingdom. But we shall recognise this, and the blessing which he means, still more clearly, if we turn to the second of the sections indicated in the previous lecture, and thereby progressively acquaint ourselves with the funda-mental features of Jesus' message.

II. *God the Father and the infinite value of the human soul.*

To our modern way of thinking and feeling, Christ's message appears in the clearest and most direct light when grasped in connexion with the idea of God the Father and the infinite value of the human soul. Here the elements which I would describe as the restful and restgiving in Jesus' message, and which are comprehended in the idea of our being children of God, find expression. I call them *restful* in contrast with the impulsive and stirring elements; although it is just they that are informed with a special strength. But the fact that the whole of Jesus' message may be reduced to these two heads—-God as the Father, and the human soul so ennobled that it can and does unite with him—shows us that the Gospel is in no-wise a positive religion like the rest; that it contains no statutory or particularistic elements; *that it is, therefore, religion itself.* It is superior to all anti-thesis and tension between this world and a world to come, between reason and ecstasy, between work and isolation from the world, between Judaism and Hellenism. It can dominate them all, and there is no factor of earthly life to which it is confined or necessarily tied down. Let us, however, get a clearer idea of what being children of God, in Jesus' sense, means, by briefly considering four groups containing sayings of his, or, as the case may be, a single saying, viz.:—(1) The Lord's Prayer; (2) that utterance, "Rejoice not that the spirits are subject unto you; but rather rejoice because your names are written in heaven"; (3) the saying, "Are not two sparrows sold for a farthing? and one of them shall not fall on the ground without your Father. But the very hairs of your head are all numbered"; (4) the utterance, "What shall it profit a man if he shall gain the whole world and lose his own soul?"

Let us take the Lord's Prayer first. It was communicated by Jesus to his disciples at a particularly solemn moment. They had asked him to teach them how to pray, as John the Baptist had taught his disciples. Thereupon he uttered the Lord's Prayer. It is by their prayers that the character of the higher religions is determined. But this prayer was spoken—as every one must feel who has ever given it a thought in his soul—by one who has overcome all inner unrest, or overcomes it the moment that he goes before God. The very apostrophe of the prayer, "Our Father," exhibits the steady faith of the man who knows that he is safe in God, and it tells us that he is certain of being heard. Not to hurl violent desires at heaven or to obtain this or that earthly blessing does he pray, but to preserve the power which he already possesses and strengthen the union with God in which he lives. No one, then, can utter this prayer unless his heart is in profound peace and his mind wholly concentrated on the inner relation of the soul with God. All other prayers are of a lower order, for they contain particularistic elements, or are so framed that in some way or other they stir the imagination in regard to the things of sense as well; whilst this prayer leads us away from everything to the height where the soul is alone with its God. And yet the earthly element is not absent. The whole of the second half of the prayer deals with earthly relations, but they are placed in the light of the Eternal. In vain will you look for any request for particular gifts of grace, or special blessings, even of a spiritual kind. "All else shall be added unto you." The name of God, His will, and His kingdom—these elements of rest and permanence are poured out over the earthly relations as well. Everything that is small and selfish melts away, and only four things are left with regard to which it is worth while to pray—the daily bread, the daily trespass, the daily temptations, and the evil in life. There is nothing in the Gospels that tells us more certainly what the Gospel is, and what sort of disposition and temper it produces, than the Lord's Prayer. With this prayer we ought also to confront all those who disparage the Gospel by representing it as an ascetic or ecstatic or sociological pronouncement. It shows the Gospel to be the Fatherhood of God applied to the whole of life; to be an inner union with God's will and God's kingdom, and a joyous certainty of the possession of eternal blessings and protection from evil.

As to the second utterance : when Jesus says "Rejoice not that the spirits are subject unto you, but rejoice rather that your names are written in heaven," it is another way of laying special emphasis on the idea that the all-important element in this religion is the consciousness of being safe in God. The greatest achievements, nay the very works which are done in the strength of this religion, fall below the assurance, at once humble and proud, of resting for time and eternity under the fatherly care of God. Moreover, the genuineness, nay the actual existence, of religious experience is to be measured, not by any transcendency of feeling nor by great deeds that all men can see, but by the joy and the peace which are diffused through the soul that can say "My Father."

How far did Christ carry this idea of the fatherly providence of God ? Here we come to the third saying : "Are not two sparrows sold for a farthing? and one of them shall not fall to the ground without your Father. But the very hairs of your head are all numbered." The assurance that God rules is to go as far as our fears go, nay, as far as life itself— life down even to its smallest manifestations in the order of nature. It was to disabuse his disciples of the fear of evil and the terrors of death that he gave them the sayings about the sparrows and the flowers of the field ; they are to learn how to see the hand of the living God everywhere in life, and in death too

Finally, in asking—and after what has gone before the question will not sound surprising—" What shall it profit a man if he shall gain the whole world and lose his own soul?" he put a man's value as high as it can be put. The man who can say " My Father" to the Being who rules heaven and earth, is thereby raised above heaven and earth, and himself has a value which is higher than all the fabric of this world. But this great saying took the stern tone of a warning. He offered them a gift and with it set them a task. How different was the Greek doctrine! Plato, it is true, had already sung the great hymn of the mind ; he had distinguished it from the whole world of appearance and maintained its eternal origin. But the mind which he meant was the knowing mind ; he contrasted it with blind, insensible matter ; his message made its appeal to the wise. Jesus Christ calls to every poor soul ; he calls to every one who bears a human face : You are children of the living God, and not only better than many sparrows but of more value than the whole world. The value of a truly great man, as I saw it put lately, consists in his increasing the value of all mankind. It is here, truly, that the highest significance of great men lies : to have enhanced, that is, to have progressively given effect to human value, to the value of that race of men which has risen up out of the dull ground of Nature. But Jesus Christ was the first to bring the value of every human soul to light, and what he did no one

can any more undo. We may take up what relation to him we will : in the history of the past no
one can refuse to recognise that it was he who
raised humanity to this level.

This highest estimate of a man's value is based
on a transvaluation of all values. To the man who
boasts of his possessions he says : " Thou fool." He
confronts everyone with the thought : " Whosoever
will lose his life shall save it." He can even say :
" He that hateth his life in this world shall keep it
unto life eternal." This is the transvaluation of
values of which many before him had a dim idea ;
of which they perceived the truth as through a veil ;
the redeeming power of which—that blessed mystery
—they felt in advance. He was the first to give
it calm, simple, and fearless expression, as though it
were a truth which grew on every tree. It was
just this that stamped his peculiar genius, that he
gave perfectly simple expression to profound and all-
important truths, as though they could not be otherwise ; as though he were uttering something that
was self-evident ; as though he were only reminding
men of what they all know already, because it lives
in the innermost part of their souls.

In the combination of these ideas—God the Father,
Providence, the position of men as God's children,
the infinite value of the human soul—the whole
Gospel is expressed. But we must recognise what
a paradox it all is ; nay, that the paradox of religion
here for the first time finds its full expression.

Measured by the experience of the senses and by exact knowledge, not only are the different religions a paradox, but so are all religious phenomena. They introduce an element, and pronounce it to be the most important of all, which is not cognisable by the senses and flies in the face of things as they are actually constituted. But all religions other than Christianity are in some way or other so bound up with the things of the world that they involve an element of earthly advantage, or, as the case may be, are akin in their substance to the intellectual and spiritual condition of a definite epoch. But what can be less obvious than the statement : the hairs of your head are all numbered ; you have a supernatural value ; you can put yourselves into the hands of a power which no one has seen ? Either that is nonsense, or else it is the utmost development of which religion is capable ; no longer a mere phenomenon accompanying the life of the senses, a coefficient, a transfiguration of certain parts of that life, but something which sets up a paramount title to be the first and the only fact that reveals the fundamental basis and meaning of life. Religion subordinates to itself the whole motley world of phenomena, and defies that world if it claims to be the only real one. Religion gives us only a single experience, but one which presents the world in a new light : the Eternal appears ; time becomes means to an end ; man is seen to be on the side of the Eternal.

This was certainly Jesus' meaning, and to take
anything from it is to destroy it.   In applying
the idea of Providence to the whole of humanity
and the world without any exception; in showing
that humanity is rooted in the Eternal; in proclaiming the fact that we are God's children as at once
a gift and a task, he took a firm grip of all fumbling
and stammering attempts at religion and brought
them to their issue.   Once more let it be said : we
may assume what position we will in regard to him
and his message, certain it is that thence onward
the value of our race is enhanced; human lives,
nay, we ourselves, have become dearer to one another.
A man may know it or not, but a real reverence for
humanity follows from the practical recognition of
God as the Father of us all.

III. *The higher righteousness and the command-*
ment of love.

This is the third head, and the whole of the
Gospel is embraced under it.   To represent the
Gospel as an ethical message is no depreciation of its
value.   The ethical system which Jesus found prevailing in his nation was both ample and profound.
To judge the moral ideas of the Pharisees solely by
their childish and casuistical aspects is not fair.   By
being bound up with religious worship and petrified
in ritual observance, the morality of holiness had,
indeed, been transformed into something that was

the clean opposite of it. But all was not yet hard and dead; there was some life still left in the deeper parts of the system. To those who questioned him Jesus could still answer: "You have the law, keep it ; you know best yourselves what you have to do ; the sum of the law is, as you yourselves say, to love God and your neighbour." Nevertheless, there is a sphere of ethical thought which is peculiarly expressive of Jesus' Gospel. Let us make this clear by citing four points.

Firstly: Jesus severed the connexion existing in his day between ethics and the external forms of religious worship and technical observance. He would have absolutely nothing to do with the purposeful and self-seeking pursuit of " good works " in combination with the ritual of worship. He exhibited an indignant contempt for those who allow their neighbours, nay, even their parents, to starve, and on the other hand send gifts to the temple. He will have no compromise in the matter. Love and mercy are ends in themselves ; they lose all value and are put to shame by having to be anything else than the service of one's neighbour.

Secondly: in all questions of morality he goes straight to the root, that is, to the disposition and the intention. It is only thus that what he calls the "higher righteousness" can be understood. The "higher righteousness" is the righteousness that will stand when the depths of the heart are probed. Here, again, we have something that is seemingly very simple and self-evident. Yet the truth, as he uttered it, took the severe form : " It was said of old . . . but I say unto you." After all, then, the truth was something new ; he was aware that it had never yet been expressed in such a consistent form and with such claims to supremacy. A large portion of the so-called Sermon on the Mount is occupied with what he says when he goes in detail through the several departments of human relationships and human failings so as to bring the disposition and intention to light in each case, to judge a man's works by them, and on them to hang heaven and hell.

Thirdly : what he freed from its connexion with self-seeking and ritual elements, and recognised as the moral principle, he reduces to *one* root and to *one* motive—love. He knows of no other, and love itself, whether it takes the form of love of one's neighbour or of one's enemy, or the love of the Samaritan, is of one kind only. It must completely fill the soul ; it is what remains when the soul dies to itself. In this sense love is the new life already begun. But it is always the love which *serves*, and only in this function does it exist and live.

Fourthly : we saw that Jesus freed the moral element from all alien connexions, even from its alliance with the public religion. Therefore to say that the Gospel is a matter of ordinary morality is not to misunderstand him. And yet there is one all-important point where he combines religion and morality. It is a point which must be felt ; it is not easy to define. In view of the Beatitudes it may, perhaps, best be described as *humility*. Jesus made love and humility one. Humility is not a virtue by itself; but it is pure receptivity, the expression of inner need, the prayer for God's grace and forgiveness, in a word, the opening up of the heart to God. In Jesus' view, this humility, which is the love of God of which we are capable—take, for instance, the parable of the Pharisee and the publican — is an abiding disposition towards the good, and that out of which everything that is good springs and grows. "Forgive us our trespasses even as we forgive them that trespass against us" is the prayer at once of humility and of love. This, then, is the source and origin of the love of one's neighbour; the poor in spirit and those who hunger and thirst after righteousness are also the peacemakers and the merciful.

It was in this sense that Jesus combined religion and morality, and in this sense religion may be called the soul of morality, and morality the body of religion. We can thus understand how it was that Jesus could place the love of God and the love of one's neighbour side by side; the love of one's neighbour is the only practical proof on earth of that love of God which is strong in humility.

In thus expressing his message of the higher righteousness and the new commandment of love in these four leading thoughts, Jesus defined the sphere of the ethical in a way in which no one before him had ever defined it. But should we be threatened with doubts as to what he meant, we must steep ourselves again and again in the Beatitudes of the Sermon on the Mount. They contain his ethics and his religion, united at the root, and freed from all external and particularistic elements.

LECTURE V.

AT the close of the last lecture 1 referred to the Beatitudes, and mentioned that they exhibit Jesus' religion in a particularly impressive way. I desire to remind you of another passage which shows that Jesus recognised the practical proof of religion to consist in the exercise of neighbourly love and mercy. In one of his last discourses he spoke of the Judgment, bringing it before his hearers' eyes in the parable of the shepherd separating the sheep from the goats. The sole principle of separation is the question of mercy. The question is raised by asking whether men gave food and drink to Jesus himself, and visited him; that is to say, it is put as a *religious* question. The paradox is then resolved in the sentence: "Inasmuch as ye have done it unto one of the least of these my brethren, ye have done it unto me." We can have no clearer illustration of the fact that in Jesus' view mercy was the quality on which everything turned, and that the temper in which it is exercised is the guarantee that a man's *religious* position is the right one. How so? Because in exercising this

virtue men are imitating God : "Be merciful, even
as your Father in heaven is merciful." He who
exercises mercy exercises God's prerogative; for
God's justice is not accomplished by keeping to
the rule, "an eye for an eye and a tooth for a
tooth," but is subject to the power of His mercy.

Let us pause here for a moment. The history of
religion marked an enormous advance, religion itself
was established afresh, when through poets and
thinkers in Greece on the one hand, and through
the prophets in Palestine on the other, the idea of
righteousness and a righteous God became a living
force and transformed tradition. The gods were
raised to a higher level and civilised; the warlike and capricious Jehovah became a holy Being
in whose court of judgment a man might trust,
albeit in fear and trembling. The two great provinces
of religion and morality, hitherto separated, were now
brought into close relation ; for " the Godhead is holy
and just." It is *our* history that was then developed ;
for without that all-important transformation there
would be no such thing as " mankind," no such thing
as a " history of the world " in the higher sense. The
most immediate result of this development may be
summed up in the maxim : " What ye would not
that men should do unto you, do ye also not unto
them." Insufficient and prosaic as the rule may
seem, yet, if extended so as to cover all human relationships and really observed, it contains a civilising
force of enormous strength.

But it does not contain the ultimate step. Not until justice was compelled to give way to mercy, and the idea of brotherhood and self-sacrifice in the service of one's neighbour became paramount—another re-establishment of religion—was the last advance accomplished that it was possible and necessary to make. Its maxim, " What ye would that men should do unto you, do ye also unto them," also seems prosaic ; and yet rightly understood it leads to the summit and comprises a new method of apprehension, and a new way of judging one's own life. The thought that "he who loses his life shall save it," runs side by side with this maxim and effects a transvaluation of values, in the certainty that a man's true life is not tied to this span of time and is not rooted in material existence.

I hope that I have thus shown, although briefly, that in the sphere of thought which is indicated by " the higher righteousness " and " the new commandment of love " Jesus' teaching is also contained in its entirety. As a matter of fact, the three spheres which we have distinguished—the kingdom of God, God as the Father and the infinite value of the human soul, and the higher righteousness showing itself in love—coalesce ; for ultimately the kingdom is nothing but the treasure which the soul possesses in the eternal and merciful God. It needs only a few touches to develop this thought into everything that, taking Jesus' sayings as its groundwork, Christendom has known and strives to maintain as hope, faith, and love.

To proceed : Now that we have established the fundamental characteristics of Jesus' message, let us try, in the second place, to treat of the main bearings of the Gospel as applied to individual problems. There are six points or questions which call for special attention, as being the most important in themselves, and consequently felt and regarded as such in all ages. And although, in the course of the Church's history, one or other of these questions may have passed into the background for a decade or two, it has always reappeared afresh, and with redoubled force :—

(1) The Gospel and the world, or the question of asceticism ;

(2) The Gospel and the poor, or the social question ;

(3) The Gospel and law, or the question of public order ;

(4) The Gospel and work, or the question of civilisation ;

(5) The Gospel and the Son of God, or the Christological question ;

(6) The Gospel and doctrine, or the question of creed.

By these six questions—the first four hang together, and the last two stand by themselves—I hope to be able to exhibit, of course only in outline, the most important bearings of Jesus' message.

(1) *The Gospel and the world, or the question
of asceticism.*

There is a widespread opinion—it is dominant in
the Catholic churches and many Protestants share it
nowadays—that, in the last resort and in the most
important things which it enjoins, the Gospel is a
strictly world-shunning and ascetic creed. Some
people proclaim this piece of intelligence with
sympathy and admiration; nay, they magnify it
into the contention that the whole value and meaning of genuine Christianity, as of Buddhism, lies in
its world-denying character. Others emphasise the
world-shunning doctrines of the Gospel in order
thereby to expose its incompatibility with modern
ethical principles, and to prove its uselessness as a
religion. The Catholic churches have found a curious
way out of the difficulty and one which is, in reality,
a product of despair. They recognise, as I have said,
the world-denying character of the Gospel, and they
teach, accordingly, that it is only in the form of
monasticism—that is, in the " vita religiosa "—that
true Christian life finds its expression. But they
admit a "lower" kind of Christianity without asceticism, as " sufficient." We will say nothing about this
strange concession now ; the Catholic doctrine is that
it is only monks who can follow Christ fully. With
this doctrine a great philosopher, and a still greater
writer, of the nineteenth century, has made common

cause. Schopenhauer extols Christianity because, and in so far as, it has produced great ascetics like St. Anthony or St. Francis; but, beyond that, every-thing in the Christian message seems to him to be useless and a stumbling-block. With a much deeper insight than Schopenhauer, and with a strength of feeling and power of language that carry us away, Tolstoi has emphasised the ascetic and world-shunning features of the Gospel, and erected them into a rule of observance. That the ascetic ideal which he de-rives from the Gospel is endowed with warmth and strength, and includes the service of one's neighbour, is a fact which we cannot deny; but to him, too, the shunning of the world is the leading character-istic of Christianity. There are thousands of our "educated" readers who find his stories suggestive and exciting, but who at the bottom of their hearts are pleased and relieved to know that Christianity means the denial of the world; for then they know very well that it does not concern them. They are certain, and rightly certain, that this world is given them to be made the best of, within the bounds of its own blessings and its own regulations; and that if Christianity makes any other claim, it thereby shows that it is unnatural. If Christianity has no goal to set before this life; if it transfers everything to a Beyond; if it declares all earthly blessings to be valueless, and points exclusively to a world-shunning and contemplative life, it is an offence to all energetic, nay, ultimately, to all true natures; for such natures are certain that our faculties are given us to be employed, and that the earth is assigned to us to be cultivated and subdued.

But is not the Gospel really a world-denying creed? Certain very well-known passages are appealed to which do not seem to admit of any other interpretation : " If thy right eye offend thee, pluck it out and cast it from thee"; "If thy right hand offend thee, cut it off"; or the answer to the rich young man : " Go and sell that thou hast, and give to the poor, and thou shalt have treasure in heaven "; or the saying about those who have made themselves eunuchs for the kingdom of heaven's sake ; or the utterance : " If any man come to me, and hate not his father, and mother, and wife, and children, and brethren and sisters, yea, and his own life also, he cannot be my disciple." These and other passages seem to settle the matter, and to prove that the Gospel is altogether world-shunning and ascetic in its character. But to this thesis I oppose three considerations which point in another direction. The first is derived from the way in which Jesus came forward, and from his manner and course of life ; the second is based upon the impression which he made upon his disciples and was reflected in their own lives ; the third springs from what we said about the fundamental features of Jesus' message.

1. We find in our Gospels a remarkable utterance by Jesus, as follows: "John came neither eating nor drinking, and they say, He hath a devil. The

Son of Man came eating and drinking, and they say,
Behold a man gluttonous and a wine-bibber." A
glutton, then, and a wine-bibber was he called in
addition to the other abusive names which were given
him. From this it clearly follows that in his whole
demeanour and manner of life he made an impression
quite different from that of the preacher of repentance on the banks of the Jordan. Towards the
various fields in which asceticism had been tradi-
tionally practised, he must have taken up an attitude of indifference. We see him in the houses of
the rich and of the poor, at meals, with women and
amongst children ; according to tradition, even at a
wedding. He allows his feet to be washed and his
head to be anointed. Further, he is glad to lodge
with Mary and Martha ; he does not ask them to
leave their home. When he finds, to his joy, people
with a firm faith, he leaves them in the calling and
the position in which they were. We do not hear
of his telling them to sell all and follow him. Apparently he thinks it possible, nay, fitting, that they
should live unto their belief in the position in which
God has placed them. His circle of disciples is not
exhausted by the few whom he summoned directly
to follow him. He finds God's children everywhere ;
to discover them in their obscurity and to be allowed
to speak to them some word of strength is his highest
pleasure. But he did not organise his disciples into
a band of monks, and he gave them no directions as
to what they were to do and leave undone in the life

of the day. No one who reads the Gospels with an unprejudiced mind, and does not pick his words, can fail to acknowledge that this free and active spirit does not appear to be bent under the yoke of asceticism, and that such words, therefore, as point in this direction must not be taken in a rigid sense and generalised, but must be regarded in a wider connexion and from a higher point of view.

2. It is certain that the disciples did not understand their master to be a world-shunning ascetic. We shall see later what sacrifices they made for the Gospel and in what sense they renounced the world. But it is evident they did not give ascetic practices the chief place; they maintained the rule that the labourer is worthy of his hire; they did not send away their wives. We are incidentally told of Peter that his wife accompanied him on his missionary journeys. Apart from what we are told of an attempt to institute a kind of communism in the congregation at Jerusalem—and we may put it aside, as it is not trustworthy and, moreover, bore no ascetic character--we find nothing in the apostolic age which suggests a community of men who were ascetics on principle; on the contrary, we find the conviction prevailing everywhere that it is within the given circumstances, in the calling and position in which he finds himself, that a man is to be a Christian. How differently things developed in Buddhism from the very start!

3. The all-important consideration is the third.

Let me remind you of what we said in regard to
Jesus' leading thoughts. In the sphere indicated
by trust in God, humanity, the forgiveness of sins
and the love of one's neighbour, there is no room
for the introduction of any other maxim, least of
all· for one of a legal character. At the same time
Jesus makes it clear in what sense the kingdom of
God is the antithesis of the world. The man who
associates any ascetic practice with the words "Take
no thought," "Be merciful even as your Father in
heaven is merciful," and so on, and puts it upon the
same level as those words, does not understand the
sublime character of these sayings, and has either
lost or has never attained the feeling that there
is a union with God in which all such questions
as shunning the world and asceticism are left far
behind.

For these reasons we must decline to regard the
Gospel as a message of world-denial.

On the other hand, Jesus speaks of three enemies,
and the watchword which he gives in dealing with
them is not that we are to flee them ; rather, he com-
mands us to annihilate them. These three enemies
are mammon, care, and selfishness. Observe that here
there is no question of flight or denial, but of a battle
which is to be fought until the enemy is annihilated ;
the forces of darkness are to be overthrown. By
mammon he understands money and worldly goods
in the widest sense of the word, worldly goods which
try to gain the mastery over us, and make us tyrants

over others; for money is "compressed force."
Jesus speaks of this enemy as if it were a person,
as if it were a knight in armour, or a king; nay,
as if it were the devil himself. It is at this enemy
that the saying, "Ye cannot serve two masters,"
is aimed. Wherever anything belonging to the
domain of mammon is of such value to a man that
he sets his heart upon it, that he trembles at the
thought of losing it, that he is no longer willing
to give it up, such a man is already in bondage.
Hence, when the Christian feels that this danger
confronts him, he is not to treat with the enemy,
but to fight, and not fight only but also destroy
the mammon. Were Christ to preach among us
to-day, he would certainly not talk in general terms,
and say to everyone, "give away everything you
have"; but there are thousands among us to whom
he would so speak, and that there is scarcely anyone
who feels compelled to apply these sayings of the
Gospel to himself is a fact that ought to make us
suspicious.

The second enemy is care. At first sight it may
surprise us that Jesus should describe care as so
terrible a foe. He ranks it with "heathenism."
It is true that in the Lord's Prayer he also taught
men to pray, "Give us this day our daily bread";
but a confident request of this kind he does not
call care. The care which he means is that which
makes us timorous slaves of the day and of material
things; the care through which bit by bit we fall

a prey to the world. Care is to him an outrage
on God, who preserves the very sparrows on the
housetop; it destroys the fundamental relation with
the Father in heaven, the childlike trust, and thus
ruins our inmost soul. This is also a point in
regard to which, as in respect to mammon, we
must confess that we do not feel deeply and strongly
enough to recognise the full truth of Jesus' message.
But the question is, Who is right—he with the
inexorable "Take no thought," or we with our
debilitating fears? We, too, in a measure feel that
a man is not really free, strong, and invincible,
until he has put aside all his cares and cast them
upon God. How much we could accomplish and
how strong we should be, if we did not fret.

And then, thirdly: selfishness. It is self-denial,
not asceticism, which Jesus requires; self-denial to
the point of self-renunciation. "If thy right eye
offend thee, pluck it out; if thy right hand offend
thee, cut it off." Wherever some desire of the
senses gains the upper hand of you, so that you
become coarse and vulgar, or in your selfishness a
new master arises in you, you must destroy it; not
because God has any pleasure in mutilation, but
because you cannot otherwise preserve your better
part. It is a hard demand. But it is not met by
any act of general renunciation, such as monks
perform—the act may leave things just as they
were before—but only by a struggle and a resolute
renunciation at the critical point.

With all these enemies, mammon, care, and selfishness, what we have to exercise is *self-denial*, and therewith the relation of Christianity to asceticism is determined. Asceticism maintains the theory that all worldly blessings are in themselves of no value. This is not the theory to which we should be led if we were to go by the Gospel; "for the earth is the Lord's, and the fulness thereof." But according to the Gospel a man is to ask : Can and ought I to regard property and honour, friends and relations as blessings, or must I put them away ? If certain of Jesus' sayings to this effect have been handed down to us in a general form and were, no doubt, so uttered, still they must be limited by the whole tenour of his discourses. What the Gospel asks of us is solemnly to examine ourselves, to maintain an earnest watch, and to destroy the enemy. There can be no doubt, however, that Jesus demanded self-denial and self-renunciation to a much greater extent than we like to think.

To sum up : Ascetic in the primary meaning of the word the Gospel is not; for it is a message of trust in God, of humility, of forgiveness of sin, and of mercy. This is a height which nothing else can approach, and into this sphere nothing else can force its way. Further, worldly blessings are not of the devil but of God—" Your heavenly Father knoweth that ye have need of all these things ; he arrays the lilies of the field and feeds the fowls of the air." Asceticism has no place in the Gospel at all ; what it

asks is that we should struggle against mammon,
against care, against selfishness; what it demands
and disengages is *love*; the love that serves and is
self-sacrificing. This struggle and this love are the
kind of asceticism which the Gospel means, and
whoever encumbers Jesus' message with any other
kind fails to understand it. He fails to understand
its grandeur and its importance; for there is something still more important than "giving one's body
to be burned and bestowing all one's goods to feed the
poor," namely, self-denial and love.

(2) *The Gospel and the poor, or the social question.*

The bearings of the Gospel in regard to the social
question form the second point which we proposed to
consider. It is closely akin to the first. Here also
we encounter different views prevalent at the present
moment, or, to be more exact, two views, which are
mutually opposed. We are told, on the one hand,
that the Gospel was in the main a great social
message to the poor, and that everything else in
it is of secondary importance—mere contemporary
wrapping, ancient tradition, or new forms supplied
by the first generations of Christians. Jesus, they
say, was a great social reformer, who aimed at re-
lieving the lower classes from the wretched condition
in which they were languishing; he set up a social
programme which embraced the equality of all men,

relief from economical distress, and deliverance from misery and oppression. It is only so, they add, that he can be understood, and therefore so he was; or perhaps—so he was, because it is only so that we can understand him. For years books and pamphlets have been written dealing with the Gospel in this sense; well-meant performances which aim at thus providing Jesus with a defence and a recommendation. But amongst those who take the Gospel to be an essentially social message there are also some who draw the opposite conclusion. By trying to prove that Jesus' message was wholly directed to bringing about an economical reform, they declare the Gospel to be an entirely Utopian and useless programme; the view, they say, which Jesus took of the world was gentle, but also weak; coming himself from the lower and oppressed classes, he shared the suspicion entertained by small people of the great and the rich; he abhorred all profitable trade and business; he failed to understand the necessity of acquiring wealth; and accordingly he shaped his programme so as to disseminate pauperism in the " world "—to him the world was Palestine—and then, by way of contrast with the misery on earth, to build up a kingdom in heaven; a programme unrealisable in itself, and offensive to men of energy. This, or something like this, is the view held by another section of those who identify the Gospel with a social message.

Opposed to this group of persons, united in the way in which they look at the Gospel but divided in their opinions in regard to it, there is another group upon whom it makes quite a different impression. They assert that as for any direct interest on Jesus' part in the economical and social conditions of his age; nay, further, as for any rudimentary interest in economical questions in general, it is only read into the Gospel, and that with economical questions the Gospel has absolutely nothing to do. Jesus, they say, certainly borrowed illustrations and examples from the domain of economics, and took a personal interest in the poor, the sick, and the miserable, but his purely religious teaching and his saving activity were in no way directed to any improvement in their earthly position : to say that his objects and intentions were of a social character is to secularize them. Nay, there are not a few among us who think him, like themselves, a "Conservative," who respected all these existing social differences and ordinances as " divinely ordained."

The voices which make themselves heard here are, as you will observe, very different, and the different points of view are defended with zeal and pertinacity. Now, if we are to try to find the position which corresponds to the facts, there is, first of all, a brief remark to be made on the age in which Jesus lived. Our knowledge of the social conditions in Palestine in his age and for some considerable time previously does not go very far; but there are certain leading features of it which we can establish, and two things more particularly which we can assert.

The governing classes, to which, above all, the Pharisees, and also the priests, belonged—the latter partly in alliance with the temporal rulers—had little feeling for the needs of the people. The condition of those classes may not have been much worse than it generally is at all times and in all nations, but it was bad. Moreover, there was here the additional circumstance that mercy and sympathy with the poor had been put into the background by devotion to public worship and to the cult of " righteousness." Oppression and tyranny on the part of the rich had long become a standing and inexhaustible theme with the Psalmists and with all men of any warm feelings. Jesus, too, could not have spoken of the rich as he did speak, unless they had grossly neglected their duties.

In the poor and oppressed classes, in the huge mass of want and evil, amongst the multitude of people for whom the word " misery" is often only another expression for the word " life," nay, is life itself—in this multitude there were groups of people at that time, as we can surely see, who, with fervent and steadfast hope, were hanging upon the promises and consoling words of their God, waiting in humility and patience for the day when their deliverance was to come. Often too poor to pay even for the barest advantages and privileges of public worship, oppressed, thrust aside, and unjustly treated, they could not raise their eyes to the temple; but they looked to the God of Israel, and fervent prayers went

up to him : " Watchman, what of the night ? "   Thus
their hearts were opened to God and ready to receive
him, and in many of the Psalms, and in the later
Jewish literature which was akin to them, the word
" poor " directly denotes those who have their hearts
open and are waiting for the consolation of Israel.
Jesus found this usage of speech in existence and
adopted it.   Therefore when we come across the
expression " the poor " in the Gospels we must not
think, without further ceremony, of the poor in the
economic sense.   As a matter of fact, poverty in the
economic sense coincided to a large extent in those
days with religious humility and an openness of the
heart towards God, in contrast with the elevated
" practice of virtue " of the Pharisees and its routine
observance in " righteousness."   But if this were the
prevailing condition of affairs, then it is clear that
our modern categories of " poor " and " rich " cannot
be unreservedly transferred to that age.   Yet we
must not forget that in those days the economical
sense was also, as a rule, included in the word " poor."
We shall, therefore, have to examine in our next
lecture the direction in which a distinction can be
made, or perhaps to ask, whether it is possible to fix
the inner sense of Jesus' words in spite of the peculiar
difficulty attaching to the conception of " poverty."
We can have some confidence, however, that we shall
not have to remain in obscurity on this point ; for in
its fundamental features the Gospel also throws a
bright light upon the field covered by this question.

LECTURE VI.

AT the close of the last lecture I referred to the problem presented by " the poor " in the Gospel. As a rule, the poor of whom Jesus was thinking were also those whose hearts are open towards God, and hence what is said of them cannot be applied without further ceremony to the poor generally. In considering the social question we must, therefore, put aside all those sayings of Jesus which obviously refer to the poor in the spiritual sense. These include, for instance, the first Beatitude, whether we accept it in the form in which it appears in Luke or in Matthew. The Beatitudes associated with it make it clear that Jesus was thinking of the poor whose hearts were inwardly open towards God. But, as we have no time to go through all the sayings separately, we must content ourselves with some leading considerations in order to establish the most important points.

Jesus regarded the possession of worldly goods as a grave danger for the soul, as hardening the heart, entangling us in earthly cares, and seducing us into a vulgar life of pleasure. "A rich man shall hardly enter the kingdom of heaven."

The contention that Jesus desired, so to speak, to bring about a general condition of poverty and distress, in order that he might afterwards make it the basis of his kingdom of heaven—a contention which we encounter in different forms—is erroneous. The very opposite is the case. Want he called want, and evil he called evil. Far from showing them any favour, he made the greatest and strongest efforts to combat and destroy them. In this sense, too, his whole activity was a saving activity, that is to say, a struggle against evil and against want. Nay, we might almost think that he over-estimated the depressing load of poverty and affliction; that he occupied himself too much with it; and that, taking the moral bearings of life as a whole, he attributed too great an importance to those forces of sympathy and mercy which are expected to counteract this state of things. But neither, of course, would this view be correct. He knows of a power which he thinks still worse than want and misery, namely, sin; and he knows of a force still more emancipating than mercy, namely, forgiveness. His discourses and actions leave no doubt upon this point. It is certain, therefore, that Jesus never and nowhere wished to keep up poverty and misery, but, on the contrary, he combated them himself and bid others combat them. The Christians who in the course of the Church's history were for countenancing mendicancy and recommending universal pauperisation, or sentimentally coquetted with misery and distress, cannot with any show of reason appeal to him. Upon those, however, who were anxious to devote their whole lives to the preaching of the Gospel and the ministry of the Word—he did not ask this of everyone, but regarded it as a special calling from God and a special gift—upon them he enjoined the renunciation of all that they had, that is to say, all worldly goods. Yet that does not mean that he relegated them to a life of beggary. On the contrary, they were to be certain that they would find their bread and their means of livelihood. What he meant by that we learn from a saying of his which was accidentally omitted from the Gospels, but has been handed down to us by the apostle Paul. In the ninth chapter of his first epistle to the Corinthians he writes: "The Lord hath ordained that they which preach the gospel should live of the gospel." An absence of worldly possessions he required of the ministers of the Word, that is, of the missionaries, in order that they might live entirely for their calling. But he did not mean that they were to beg. This is a Franciscan misconception which is perhaps suggested by Jesus' words but carries us away from his meaning.

In this connexion allow me to digress for a moment from our subject. Those members of the Christian churches who have become professional evangelists or ministers of the Word in their parishes have not, as a rule, found it necessary to follow the Lord's injunction to dispossess themselves of their worldly goods. So far as priests or pastors, as the case may be, and not missionaries, are concerned, it may be said with some justice that the injunction does not refer to them; for it presupposes that a man has undertaken the office of *propagating* the Gospel. It may be said, further, that the Lord's injunctions, over and above those relating to the commandment of love, must not be made into inviolable laws, as otherwise Christian liberty will be impaired, and the high privilege of the Christian religion to adapt its shape to the course of history, free from all constraint, will be prejudiced. But still it may be asked whether it would not have been an extraordinary gain to Christianity if those who are called to be its ministers,—the missionaries and pastors, had followed the Lord's rules. At the very least, it ought to be a strict principle with them to concern themselves with property and worldly goods only so far as will prevent them being a burden to others, and beyond that to renounce them. I entertain no doubt that the time will come when the world will tolerate a life of luxury among those who are charged with the cure of souls as little as it tolerates priestly government. Our feelings in this respect are becoming finer, and that is an advantage. It will no longer be thought fitting, in the higher sense of the word, for anyone to preach resignation and contentment to the poor, who is well off himself, and zealously concerned for the increase of his property. A healthy man may well offer consolation to the sick; but how shall a man of property convince those who have none that worldly goods are of no value? The Lord's injunction that the minister of the Word is to divest himself of worldly possessions will still come to be honoured in the history of his communion.

Jesus laid down no social programme for the suppression of poverty and distress, if by programme we mean a set of definitely prescribed regulations. With economical conditions and contemporary circumstances he did not interfere. Had he become entangled in them; had he given laws which were ever so salutary for Palestine, what would have been gained by it? They would have served the needs of a day, and to-morrow would have been antiquated; to the Gospel they would have been a burden and a source of confusion. We must be careful not to exceed the limits set to such injunctions as "Give to him that asketh thee" and others of a similar kind. They must be understood in connexion with the time and the situation. They refer to the immediate wants of the applicant, which were satisfied with a piece of bread, a drink of water, an article of clothing to cover his nakedness. We must remember that in the Gospel we are in the East, and in circumstances which from an economical point of view are somewhat undeveloped. Jesus was no social

reformer. He could say on occasion, "The poor ye
have always with you," and thereby, it seems,
indicate that the conditions would undergo no
essential change. He refused to be a judge between
contending heirs, and a thousand problems of economics and social life he would have just as resolutely put aside as the unreasonable demand that he
would settle a question of inheritance. Yet again and
again people have ventured to deduce some concrete
social programme from the Gospel. Even evangelical
theologians have made the attempt, and are still
making it—an endeavour hopeless in itself and full
of danger, but absolutely bewildering and intolerable when people try to "fill up the gaps"—and
they are many—to be found in the Gospel with
regulations and programmes drawn from the Old
Testament.

No religion, not even Buddhism, ever went to
work with such an energetic social message, and so
strongly identified itself with that message as we
see to be the case in the Gospel. How so? Because
the words "Love thy neighbour as thyself" were
spoken in deep earnest; because with these words
Jesus turned a light upon all the concrete relations
of life, upon the world of hunger, poverty and misery ;
because, lastly, he uttered them as a religious, nay,
as *the* religious maxim. Let me remind you once
more of the parable of the Last Judgment, where the
whole question of a man's worth and destiny is made
dependent on whether he has practised the love of

his neighbour ; let me remind you of the other parable of the rich man and poor Lazarus. I should like to cite another story, too, which is little known, because it occurs in this wording not in our four Gospels but in the Gospel of the Hebrews. The story of the rich young man is there handed down as follows :—" A rich man said to the Lord : Master, what good must I do that I may have life ? He answered him : Man, keep the law and the prophets. The other answered : That have I done. He said to him : Go, sell all thy possessions and distribute them to the poor, and come and follow me. Then the rich man began to scratch his head, and the speech did not please him. And the Lord said to him : How canst thou say : I have kept the law and the prophets, as it is written in the law, Love thy neighbour as thyself ? Behold, many of thy brethren, sons of Abraham, lie in dirty rags and die of hunger, and thy house is full of many goods, and nothing comes out of it to them." You observe how Jesus felt the material wants of the poor, and how he deduced a remedy for such distress from the commandment : " Love thy neighbour as thyself." People ought not to speak of loving their neighbours if they can allow men beside them to starve and die in misery. It is not only that the Gospel preaches solidarity and the helping of others ; it is in this message that its real import consists. In this sense it is profoundly socialistic, just as it is also profoundly individualistic, because it establishes the infinite and independent

value of every human soul. Its tendency to union
and brotherliness is not so much an accidental phenomenon in its history as the essential feature of its
character. The Gospel aims at founding a community among men as wide as human life itself and
as deep as human need. As has been truly said, its
object is to transform the socialism which rests on
the basis of conflicting interests into the socialism
which rests on the consciousness of a spiritual unity.
In this sense its social message can never be outbid.
In the course of the ages people's opinions as to
what constitutes "an existence worthy of a man"
have, thank God, become much changed and im-
proved. But Jesus, too, knew of this way of
measuring things. Did he not once refer, almost
bitterly, to his own position : "The foxes have holes,
and the birds of the air have nests : but the Son of
Man hath not where to lay his head" ? A dwelling,
sufficient daily bread, cleanliness—all these needs
he touched upon, and their satisfaction he held to be
necessary, and a condition of earthly life. If a man
cannot procure them for himself, others are to step
in and do it for him. There can be no doubt, therefore, that if Jesus were with us to-day he would side
with those who are making great efforts to relieve
the hard lot of the poor and procure them better
conditions of life. The fallacious principle of the free
play of forces, of the "live and let live" principle—
a better name for it would be the "live and let die"—
is entirely opposed to the Gospel. And it is not as our

servants, but as our brothers, that we are to help the poor.

Lastly, our riches do not belong to us alone. The Gospel has prescribed no regulations as to how we are to use them, but it leaves us in no doubt that we are to regard ourselves not as owners but as administrators in the service of our neighbour. Nay, it almost looks as if Jesus contemplated the possibility of a union among men in which wealth, as private property in the strict sense of the word, was non-existent. Here, however, we touch upon a question which is not easy to decide, and which, perhaps, ought not to be raised at all, because Jesus' eschatological ideas and his particular horizon enter into it. Nor is it a question that we need raise. It is the disposition which Jesus kindled in his disciples towards poverty and want that is all-important.

The Gospel is a social message, solemn and overpowering in its force; it is the proclamation of solidarity and brotherliness, in favour of the poor. But the message is bound up with the recognition of the infinite value of the human soul, and is contained in what Jesus said about the kingdom of God. We may also assert that it is an essential part of what he there said. But laws or ordinances or injunctions bidding us forcibly alter the conditions of the age in which we may happen to be living are not to be found in the Gospel.

(3) *The Gospel and the law, or the question
of public order.*

The problem dealing with the relation of the
Gospel to law embraces two leading questions: (1)
the relation of the Gospel to constituted authority;
(2) the relation of the Gospel to legal ordinances
generally, in so far as they possess a wider range
than is covered by the conception "constituted
authority." It is not easy to mistake the answer
to the first question, but the second is more complicated and beset with greater difficulties; and
very diverse opinions are entertained in regard
to it.

As to Jesus' relation to the constituted authorities of his day, I need scarcely remind you again
in express terms that he was no political revolutionary, and that he laid down no political programme. Although he is sure that his Father
would send him twelve legions of angels were he
to ask Him, he did not ask Him. When they
wanted to make him a king, he disappeared. Ultimately, indeed, when he thought well to reveal
himself to the whole nation as the Messiah—how
he came to the decision and carried it out are
points in which we are left in the dark—he made
his entry into Jerusalem as a king; but of the modes
of presenting himself which prophecy suggested,
he chose that which was most remote from

a political manifestation. The way in which he understood his Messianic duty is shown by his driving the buyers and sellers from the temple. In this cleansing of the temple it was not the constituted authorities whom he attacked, but those who had assumed to themselves rights of authority over the soul. In every nation, side by side with the constituted authorities, an unconstituted authority is established, or rather two unconstituted authorities. They are the political church and the political parties. What the political church wants, in the widest sense of the word and under very various guises, is to rule; to get hold of men's souls and bodies, consciences and worldly goods. What political parties want is the same; and when the heads of these parties set themselves up as popular leaders, a terrorism is developed which is often worse than the fear of royal despots. It was not otherwise in Palestine in Jesus' day. The priests and the Pharisees held the nation in bondage and murdered its soul. For this unconstituted "authority" Jesus showed a really emancipating and refreshing disrespect. He was never tired of attacking it—nay, in his struggle with it he roused himself to a state of holy indignation—of exposing its wolfish nature and hypocrisy, and of declaring that its day of judgment was at hand. In whatever domain it had any warrant to act, he accepted it: "Go and show yourselves unto the priests." So far as they really proclaimed God's law he recognised them : "Whatever they tell you to do, that do." But these were the people to whom he read the terrible lecture given in Matthew xxiii.: "Woe unto you, scribes and Pharisees, hypocrites! for ye are like unto whited sepulchres, which indeed appear beautiful outward, but are within full of dead men's bones and of all uncleanness." Towards these spiritual "authorities," then, he filled his disciples with a holy want of respect, and even of "King" Herod he spoke with bitter irony : "Go ye and tell that fox." On the other hand, so far as we can judge from the scanty evidence before us, his attitude towards the real authorities, those who wielded the sword, was different. He recognised that they had an actual right to be obeyed, and he never withdrew his own person from their jurisdiction. Nor are we to understand the commandment against swearing as including an oath taken before a magistrate. No one with a grain of salt, as Wellhausen has rightly said, can miss the inner meaning of this commandment. On the other hand, we must be careful not to rate Jesus' position in regard to constituted authority too high. People usually appeal to the often quoted saying : "Render unto Cæsar the things which are Cæsar's and unto God the things that are God's." But this saying is often misunderstood. Wherever it is explained as meaning that Jesus recognised God and Cæsar as the two powers which in some way or other exist side by side, or are even in secret alliance, it is taken in a wrong sense. Jesus had no such thought; on the contrary, he spoke of the two powers as separate and divorced from each other. God and Cæsar are the lords of two quite different provinces. Jesus settled the question that was in dispute by pointing out this difference, which is so great that no conflict between the powers can arise. The penny is an earthly coin and bears Cæsar's image; let it be given, then, to Cæsar, but—this we may take as the complement—the soul and all its powers have nothing to do with Cæsar; they belong to God. In a word, the all-important matter, in Jesus' view, is not to mix up the two provinces. When we are once quite clear about this, then we may go on to remark on the significance of the fact that Jesus enjoined compliance with the demand for payment of the imperial taxes. No doubt it is important to note that he himself respected the constituted authorities, and wished to see them respected; but in regard to the estimate which he formed of them, what he said is, at the least, of a neutral character.

On the other hand, we possess another saying of Jesus in regard to constituted authority which is much less often quoted, and nevertheless affords us a deeper insight into the Lord's thoughts than the one which we have just discussed. Let us consider it for a moment. The fact that it forms a point of transition to the

consideration of the attitude which Jesus took up in
regard to legal regulations in general also makes it
worth our attention. In Mark x. 42, we read:
" Jesus called them (*i.e.* his disciples) to him and
saith unto them, Ye know that they which are
accounted to rule over the Gentiles exercise lordship
over them : and their great ones exercise authority
upon them. But so shall it not be among you :
but whosoever shall be great among you shall be your
minister : and whosoever of you will be the chiefest
shall be servant of all." Observe here, first of all, the
" transvaluation of values." Jesus simply reverses the
usual process: to be great and to occupy the foremost
position means, in his view, to serve ; his disciples are
to aim, not at ruling, but at each being all other men's
servant. Next observe the opinion which he has
of authority as it was then constituted. Their
functions are based on *force*, and this is the very
reason which, in Jesus' view, puts them outside
the moral sphere ; nay, there is a fundamental
opposition between it and them : " Thus do the
earthly rulers." Jesus tells his disciples to act
differently. Law and legal ordinance, as resting
on force only, on actual power and its exercise,
have no moral value. Nevertheless Jesus did not
command men not to subject themselves to these
authorities ; they were to rate them according to
their value, that is, according to their non-value,
and they were to arrange their own lives on other
principles, namely, on the opposite ; they were not

to use force, but to serve. Here we have already
passed to the general ground of legal ordinance, for
it seems to be an essential feature of all law to secure
observance by force when called in question.

When we approach the second point, the relation
of the Gospel to legal ordinance generally, we again
encounter two different views. One of them—
in modern times more particularly maintained, in
his treatise on Canon Law, by Prof. Sohm of Leipzig,
who presents points of contact with Tolstoi—lays
down that in their respective natures law and the
world of spiritual things are diametrically opposed ;
and that it is in contradiction with the character
of the Gospel and the community founded thereon
that the Church has developed any legal ordinances
at all. In his survey of the earliest development
of the Church Prof. Sohm has gone so far as to
see in the moment when Christendom gave a
place in its midst to legal ordinances a second Fall.
Nevertheless he is unwilling to impugn the law
in its own province. But Tolstoi refuses, in the
name of the Gospel, to allow the law any rights
at all. He maintains that the leading principle
of the Gospel is that a man is never to insist upon
his rights, and that not even constituted authority
is to offer any external resistance to evil. Authority
and law are simply to cease. Opposed to Tolstoi
there are others who more or less positively contend
that the Gospel takes law and legal relations under
its protection ; that it sanctifies them and thereby

raises them into a divine sphere. These are, briefly, the two leading points of view which are here in conflict.

As regards the latter, there is little that need be said. It is a mockery of the Gospel to say that it protects and sanctifies everything that presents itself as law and legal relation at a given moment. Leaving a thing alone and bearing with it are not the same as sanctioning and preserving it. Nay, it is a serious question whether even bearing with it is not too much to say, and whether Tolstoi is not right. The difficulty of the matter makes it necessary that I should take you back a little way in Jewish history.

For hundreds of years the poor and oppressed in the people of Israel had been crying out for justice. It was a cry which still affects us to-day as we hear it in the words of the prophets and out of the prayers of the Psalmists; but time after time it passed unheeded. None of the legal regulations in force was free from the power of tyrannical authorities, to be distorted and exploited by them just as they saw fit. In speaking of legal regulations and their exercise, and in examining Jesus' attitude towards them, we must not straightway think of our own legal relations, which have grown up partly on the basis of Christianity. Jesus was of a nation the greater part of which had for generations been in vain asking for their rights, and which was familiar with law only in the form

of force. The necessary consequence was that in
such a nation a feeling of despair arose in regard
to the law ; despair, as much of the possibility of
ever getting justice on earth as, conversely, of the
moral claim of law to have any validity at all.
We can see something of this temper even in the
Gospel. But there is a second consideration which
is a standing corrective to this temper. Jesus, like
all truly religious minds, was firmly convinced that
in the end God will do justice. If He does not do
it here, He will do it in the Beyond, and that is
the main point. In this connexion there was,
in Jesus' view, nothing objectionable in the idea
of law in the sense of a just recompense ; it was a
lofty, nay, a dominating idea. Just recompense is
the function of God's majesty ; to what extent it
is modified by His mercy is a question which we
need not here consider. The contention that Jesus
took a depreciatory view of law as such, and of the
exercise of law, cannot be sustained for a moment.
On the contrary, everyone is to get his rights ;
nay more, his disciples are one day to share in
administering God's justice and themselves judge.
It was only the justice which was exercised with
violence and therefore unjustly, the justice which
lay upon the nation like a tyrannical and bloody
decree,. that he set aside. He believed in true
justice, and he was certain, too, that it would
prevail ; so certain, that he did not think it necessary for justice to use force in order to remain justice.

This brings us to the last point. We possess a number of Jesus' sayings in which he directs his disciples to renounce all their lawful demands, and so forego their just rights. You all know those sayings. Let me remind you of one only: "But I say unto you, That ye resist not evil, but whosoever shall smite thee on thy right cheek, turn to him the other also. And if any man will sue thee at the law, and take away thy coat, let him have thy cloak also." The demand here made seems to proscribe law and disorganise all the legal relations of life. Again and again these words have been appealed to with the object of showing either that Christianity is incompatible with life as it actually is, or that Christendom has fallen away from the principles of its Master. By way of reply to this argument the following observations may be made:—(i.) Jesus was, as we have seen, steeped in the conviction that God does justice; in the end, therefore, the oppressor will not prevail, but the oppressed will get his rights. (ii.) Earthly rights are in themselves of little account, and it does not much matter if we lose them. (iii.) The world is in such an unhappy state, injustice has got so much the upper hand in it, that the victim of oppression is incapable of making good his rights even if he tries. (iv.) As God—and this is the main point—mingles His justice with mercy, and lets His sun shine on the just and on the unjust, so Jesus' disciple is to show love to his enemies and disarm them by gentleness. Such are the thoughts which underlie those lofty sayings and at the same time set them their due limits. And is the demand which they contain really so supramundane, so impossible? Do we not in the circle of our family and friends advise those who belong to us to act in the same way, and not to return evil for evil and abuse for abuse? What family, what society, could continue to exist, if every member of it were anxious only to pursue his own rights, and did not learn to renounce them even when attacked? Jesus regards his disciples as a circle of friends, and he looks out beyond this circle to a league of brothers which will take shape in the future and extend. But, we are asked, are we in all cases to renounce the pursuit of our rights in the face of our enemies? are we to use no weapons but those of gentleness? To speak with Tolstoi, are the magistrates not to inflict punishment, and thereby to be effaced? are nations not to fight for house and home when they are wantonly attacked? I venture to maintain that, when Jesus spoke the words which I have quoted, he was not thinking of such cases, and that to interpret them in this direction involves a clumsy and dangerous misconception of their meaning. Jesus never had anyone but the individual in mind, and the abiding disposition of the heart in love. To say that this disposition cannot coexist with the pursuit of one's own rights, with the conscientious administration of justice, and with the stern punishment of crime, is a piece of prejudice, in support of which we may appeal in vain to the letter of those sayings, which did not aim at being laws or, therefore, at prescribing regulations. This much, however, must be added, in order that the loftiness of the demand which the Gospel makes may be in no way abated : Jesus' disciple ought to be able to renounce the pursuit of his rights, and ought to co-operate in forming a nation of brothers, in which justice is done, no longer by the aid of force, but by free obedience to the good, and which is united not by legal regulations but by the ministry of love.

LECTURE VII.

WE were occupied in the last lecture with the relation of the Gospel to law and legal ordinance. We saw that Jesus was convinced that God does, and will do, justice. We saw, further, that he demanded of his disciples that they should be able to renounce their rights. In giving expression to this demand, far from having all the circumstances of his own time in mind, still less the more complex conditions of a later age, he has one and one only present to his soul, namely, the relation of every man to the kingdom of God. Because a man is to sell all that he has in order to buy the pearl of great price, so he must also be able to abandon his earthly rights and subordinate everything to that highest relation. But in connexion with this message of his, Jesus opens up to us the prospect of a union among men, which is held together not by any legal ordinance, but by the rule of love, and where a man conquers his enemy by gentleness. It is a high and glorious ideal, and we have received it from the very foundation of our religion. It ought to float before our eyes as the goal and guiding star of our historical development.

Whether mankind will ever attain to it, who can say ?
but we can and ought to approximate to it, and in
these days—otherwise than two or three hundred
years ago—we feel a moral obligation in this
direction. Those of us who possess more delicate
and therefore more prophetic perceptions no longer
regard the kingdom of love and peace as a mere
Utopia.

But for this very reason there are many among
us to-day upon whom a very serious and difficult
question presses with redoubled force. We see a
whole class struggling for its rights ; or, rather, we
see it struggling to extend and increase its rights.
Is that compatible with the Christian temper ? Does
not the Gospel forbid such a struggle ? Have we not
been told that we are to renounce the rights we have,
to say nothing of trying to get more ? Must we,
then, as Christians, recall the labouring classes from
the struggle for their rights, and exhort them only
to patience and submission ?

The problem with which we have here to do is also
stated more or less in the form of an accusation against
Christianity. Earnest men in political circles of a
socialistic tendency, who would gladly be guided by
Jesus Christ, complain that in this matter the Gospel
leaves them in the lurch. They say that it imposes
restraint upon aspirations which with a clear conscience they feel to be justified ; that in requiring
absolute meekness and submission it disarms everyone who wants to fight ; that it narcotises, as it were,

all real energy. Some say this with pain and regret,
others with satisfaction. The latter assert that they
always knew that the Gospel was not for the healthy
and the strong, but for the broken-down ; that it
knows, and wants to know, nothing of the fact that
life, and especially modern life, is a struggle, a
struggle for one's own rights. What answer are we
to give them ?

My own opinion is that these statements and
complaints are made by people who have never yet
clearly realised with what it is that the Gospel has to
do, and who rashly and improperly connect it with
earthly things. The Gospel makes its appeal to the
inner man, who, whether he is well or wounded, in
a happy position or a miserable, obliged to spend
his earthly life fighting or quietly maintaining what
he has won, always remains the same. " My kingdom
is not of this world " ; it is no earthly kingdom that
the Gospel establishes. These words not only exclude
such a political theocracy as the Pope aims at setting
up and all worldly dominion, they have a much
wider range. Negatively they forbid all direct and
formal interference of religion in worldly affairs.
Positively what the Gospel says is this : Whoever
you may be, and whatever your position, whether
bondman or free, whether fighting or at rest—your
real task in life is always the same. There is only
one relation and *one* idea which you must not violate,
and in the face of which all others are only transient
wrappings and vain show : to be a child of God and

a citizen of His kingdom, and to exercise love. How you are to maintain yourself in this life on earth, and in what way you are to serve your neighbour, is left to you and your own liberty of action. This is what the apostle Paul understood by the Gospel, and I do not believe that he misunderstood it. Then let us fight, let us struggle, let us get justice for the oppressed, let us order the circumstances of the world as we with a clear conscience can, and as we may think best for our neighbour; but do not let us expect the Gospel to afford us any direct help; let us make no selfish demands for ourselves; and let us not forget that the world passes away, not only with the lusts thereof, but also with its regulations and its goods! Once more be it said: the Gospel knows only one goal, one idea; and it demands of a man that he shall never put them aside. If the exhortation to renounce takes, in a harsh and onesided way, a foremost place in Jesus' words, we must be careful to keep before our eyes the paramount and exclusive claims of the relation to God and the idea of love. The Gospel is above all questions of mundane development; it is concerned not with material things but with the souls of men.

With this we have already passed to the next question which was to occupy our attention, and we have half answered it.

(4) *The Gospel and work, or the question of
civilisation.*

The points which we shall have to consider here
are essentially the same as those which we emphasized
in regard to the question just discussed; and we
shall therefore be able to proceed more concisely.

Jesus' teaching has been felt again and again, but
above all in our own day, to exhibit no interest in
any systematic work or calling, and no appreciation
of those ideal possessions which go by the name of
Art and Science.   Nowhere, people say, does Jesus
summon men to labour and to put their hands to the
work of progress; in vain shall we look in his words
for any expression of pleasure in vigorous activity;
these ideal possessions lay far beyond his field of
vision.   In that last, unhappy book of his, *The Old
Faith and the New*, David Friedrich Strauss gave
particularly harsh expression to this feeling.   He
speaks of a fundamental defect in the Gospel, which
he considers antiquated and useless because out
of sympathy with the progress of civilisation.   But
long before Strauss the Pietistic movement exhibited
the same sort of feeling.   The Pietists tried to evade
the difficulty in a way of their own.   They started
from the position that Jesus must be able to serve as
a direct example for all men, whatever their calling;
that he must have proved himself in all the situations
in which a man can be placed.   They admitted that

a cursory examination of Jesus' life disclosed the fact
that this requirement was not fulfilled; but they
were of opinion that on a closer inspection it would
be found that he was really the best bricklayer, the
best tailor, the best judge, the best scholar, and so
on, and that he had the best knowledge and understanding for everything. They turned and twisted
what Jesus said and did until it was made to express
and corroborate what they wanted. Although it was
a childish attempt which they made, the problem of
which they were sensible was nevertheless of some
moment. They felt that their consciences and their
callings bound them to a definite activity and a
definite business; they were clear that they ought
not to become monks; and yet they were anxious to
practise the imitation of Christ in the full sense.
They felt, then, that he must have stood in the same
situation as they themselves, and that his horizon
must have been the same as theirs.

Here we have the same case as we dealt with in
the last section, only covering a wider field. It is
the ancient and constantly recurring error, that the
Gospel has to do with the affairs of the world, and
that it is its business to prescribe how they are to
be carried on. Here, too, the old and almost in-
eradicable tendency of mankind to rid itself of its
freedom and responsibility in higher things and
subject itself to a law, comes into play. It is much
easier, in fact, to resign oneself to any, even the
sternest, kind of authority, than to live in the liberty

of the good.   But apart from this, the question
remains : Is it not a real defect in the Gospel that
it betrays so little sympathy with the business of
life, and is out of touch with the *humaniora* in the
sense of science, art, and civilisation generally ?

I answer, in the first place : What would have
been gained if it had not possessed this " defect " ?
Suppose that it had taken an active interest in all
those efforts, would it not have become entangled
in them, or, at any rate, have incurred the risk
of appearing to be so entangled ?   Labour, art,
science, the progress of civilisation—these are not
things which exist in the abstract ; they exist in
the particular phase of an age.   The Gospel, then,
would have had to ally itself with them.   But phases
change.   In the Roman Church of to-day we see
how heavily religion is burdened by being connected with a particular epoch of civilisation.
In the Middle Ages this Church, anxious to participate to the full in all questions of progress and
civilisation, gave them form and shape, and laid
down their laws.   Insensibly, however, the Church
identified its sacred inheritance and its peculiar
mission with the knowledge, the maxims, and the
interests which it then acquired ; so that it is now,
as it were, firmly pinned down to the philosophy,
the political economy, in short, to the whole
civilisation, of the Middle Ages.   On the other
hand, what a service the Gospel has rendered to
mankind by having sounded the notes of re-

ligion in mighty chords and banished every other melody!

In the second place, labour and the progress of civilisation are, no doubt, very precious, and summon us to strenuous exertion. But they do not comprise the highest ideal. They are incapable of filling the soul with real satisfaction. Although work may give pleasure, that is only one aspect of the matter. I have always found that the people who talk loudest about the pleasure which work affords make no very great efforts themselves; whilst those who are uninterruptedly engaged in heavy labour are hesitating in its praises. As a matter of fact, there is a great deal of hypocritical twaddle talked about work. Three-fourths of it and more is nothing but stupefying toil, and the man who really works hard shares the poet's aspirations as he looks forward to evening:

Head, hands and feet rejoice: the work is done.

And, then, think of the results of all this labour! When a man has done a piece of work, he would like to do it over again, and the knowledge of its defects falls heavily on soul and conscience. No! it is not in so far as we work that we live, but in so far as we rejoice in the love of others, and ourselves exercise love. Faust is right: Labour which is labour and nothing else becomes an aversion. We long for the streams of living water, and for the spring itself from which those waters flow:

Man sehnt sich nach des Lebens Bächen,
Ach! nach des Lebens Quelle hin.

Labour is a valuable safety-valve and useful in keeping off greater ills, but it is not in itself an absolute good, and we cannot include it amongst our ideals. The same may be said of the progress of civilisation. It is of course to be welcomed; but the piece of progress in which we delight to-day becomes something mechanical by to-morrow, and leaves us cold. The man of any deep feeling will thankfully receive anything that the development of progress may bring him; but he knows very well that his situation inwardly — the problems that agitate him and the fundamental position in which he stands—is not essentially, nay is scarcely even unessentially, altered by it all. It is only for a moment that it seems as if something new were coming, and a man were being really relieved of his burden. Gentlemen, when a man grows older and sees more deeply into life, he does not find, if he possesses any inner world at all, that he is advanced by the external march of things, by " the progress of civilisation." Nay, he feels himself, rather, where he was before, and forced to seek the sources of strength which his forefathers also sought. He is forced to make himself a native of the kingdom of God, the kingdom of the Eternal, the kingdom of Love; and he comes to understand that it was only of this kingdom that Jesus Christ desired to speak and to testify, and he is grateful to him for it.

But, in the third place, Jesus had a strong and
positive conviction of the aggressive and forward
character of his message. " I am come to send fire
on the earth, and "—he added—" what will I if it
be already kindled ? " The fire of the judgment and
the forces of love were what he wanted to summon
up, so as to create a new humanity. If he spoke
of these forces of love in the simple manner corresponding to the conditions nearest at hand—the
feeding of the hungry, the clothing of the naked, the
visiting of the sick and those in prison—it is nevertheless clear that a great inward transformation of
the humanity which he saw in the mirror of the
little nation in Palestine hovered before his eyes :
" One is your master, and all ye are brethren." The
last hour is come ; but in the last hour from a small
seed a tree is to grow up which shall spread its
branches far and wide. Further, he was revealing the
knowledge of God, and he was certain that it would
ripen the young, strengthen the weak, and make
them God's champions. Knowledge of God is the
spring that is to fructify the barren field, and pour
forth streams of living water. In this sense he spoke
of it as the highest and the only necessary good,
as the condition of all edification, and, we may also
say, of all true growth and progress. Lastly, he saw
on his horizon not only the judgment, but also
a kingdom of justice, of love, and of peace, which,
though it came from heaven, was nevertheless for
this earth. When it is to come, he himself knows

not—the hour is known to the Father only; but he knows how and by what means it will spread ; and side by side with the highly-coloured, dramatic pictures which pass through his soul there are quiet perceptions which are fixed and steady. He sees the vineyard of God on this earth and God calling His labourers into it—happy the man who receives a call ! They labour in the vineyard, stand no longer idle in the market-place, and at last receive their reward. Or take the parable of the talents distributed in order to be employed, and therefore not to be buried in a napkin. A day's work, labour, increase, progress—he sees it all, but placed at the service of God and neighbour, encircled by the light of the Eternal, and removed from the service of transient things.

To sum up what we have here tried to indicate : Is the complaint from which we started at the beginning of this section justified ? Ought we really to desire that the Gospel had adapted itself to "the progress of civilisation"? Here too, I think, we have to learn from the Gospel and not to find fault with it. It tells us of the real work which humanity has to accomplish, and we ought not to meet its message by entrenching ourselves behind our miserable " work of civilisation." " The image of Christ," as a modern historian justly says, " remains the sole basis of all moral culture, and in the measure in which it succeeds in making its light penetrate is the moral culture of the nations increased or diminished."

(5) *The Gospel and the Son of God, or the Christological question.*

We now pass from the sphere of questions of which we have been treating hitherto. The four previous questions are all intimately connected with one another. Failure to answer them rightly always proceeds from not rating the Gospel high enough; from somehow or other dragging it down to the level of mundane questions and entangling it in them. Or, to put the matter differently: The forces of the Gospel appeal to the deepest foundations of human existence and to them only; it is there alone that their leverage is applied. If a man is unable, then, to go down to the root of humanity, and has no feeling for it and no knowledge of it, he will fail to understand the Gospel, and will then try to profane it or else complain that it is of no use.

We now, however, approach quite a different problem: What position did Jesus himself take up towards the Gospel while he was proclaiming it, and how did he wish himself to be accepted? We are not yet dealing with the way in which his disciples accepted him, or the place which they gave him in their hearts, and the opinion which they formed of him; we are now speaking only of his own testimony of himself. But the question is one which lands us in the great sphere of controverted questions which cover the history of the Church

from the first century up to our own time. In
the course of this controversy men put an end to
brotherly fellowship for the sake of a *nuance*; and
thousands were cast out, condemned, loaded with
chains and done to death. It is a gruesome story.
On the question of "Christology" men beat their
religious doctrines into terrible weapons, and spread
fear and intimidation everywhere. This attitude
still continues : Christology is treated as though the
Gospel had no other problem to offer, and the accompanying fanaticism is still rampant in our own
day. Who can wonder at the difficulty of the
problem, weighed down as it is with such a burden
of history and made the sport of parties? Yet anyone who will look at our Gospels with unprejudiced
eyes will not find that the question of Jesus' own
testimony is insoluble. So much of it, however, as
remains obscure and mysterious to our minds ought
to remain so; as Jesus meant it to be, and as in
the very nature of the problem it is. It is only in
pictures that we can give it expression. "There
are phenomena which cannot, without the aid of
symbols, be brought within the range of the understanding."

Before we examine Jesus' own testimony about
himself, two leading points must be established.
In the first place, he desired no other belief in his
person and no other attachment to it than is contained in the keeping of his commandments. Even
in the fourth Gospel, in which Jesus' person often

seems to be raised above the contents of the Gospel, the idea is still clearly formulated : " If ye love me, keep my commandments." He must himself have found, during his labours, that some people honoured, nay, even trusted him, without troubling themselves about the contents of his message. It was to them that he addressed the reprimand : " Not everyone that saith unto me Lord, Lord, shall enter into the kingdom of Heaven ; but he that doeth the will of my Father." To lay down any "doctrine" about his person and his dignity independently of the Gospel was, then, quite outside his sphere of ideas. In the second place, he described the Lord of heaven and earth as his God and his Father ; as the Greater, and as Him who is alone good. He is certain that everything which he has and everything which he is to accomplish comes from this Father. He prays to Him ; he subjects himself to His will ; he struggles hard to find out what it is and to fulfil it. Aim, strength, understanding, the issue, and the hard *must*, all come from the Father. This is what the Gospels say, and it cannot be turned and twisted. This feeling, praying, working, struggling and suffering individual is a man who in the face of his God also associates himself with other men.

These two facts mark out, as it were, the boundaries of the ground covered by Jesus' testimony of himself. They do not, it is true, give us any positive information as to what he said ; but we shall understand what he really meant by his testimony if we look closely at the two descriptions which he gave of himself: the *Son of God* and the *Messiah* (the Son of David, the Son of Man).

The description of himself as the Son of God, Messianic though it may have been in its original conception, lies very much nearer to our modern way of thinking than the other, for Jesus himself gave a meaning to this conception which almost takes it out of the class of messianic ideas, or at all events does not make its inclusion in that class necessary to a proper understanding of it. On the other hand, if we do not desire to be put off with a lifeless word, the description of himself as the Messiah is at first blush one that is quite foreign to our ideas. Without some explanation we cannot understand, nay, unless we are Jews, we cannot understand at all, what this post of honour means and what rank and character it possesses. It is only when we have ascertained its meaning by historical research that we can ask whether the word has a significance which in any way survives the destruction of the husk in which it took shape in Jewish political life.

Let us first of all consider the designation, "Son of God." Jesus in one of his discourses made it specially clear why and in what sense he gave himself this name. The saying is to be found in Matthew, and not, as might perhaps have been expected, in John : "No man knoweth the Son but the Father; neither knoweth any man the

Father, save the Son, and he to whomsoever the
Son will reveal him." It is "knowledge of God"
that makes the sphere of the Divine Sonship. It
is in this knowledge that he came to know the
sacred Being who rules heaven and earth as Father,
as *his* Father. The consciousness which he possessed of being *the Son of God* is, therefore, nothing but the practical consequence of knowing God
as the Father and as his Father. Rightly understood, the name of Son means nothing but the
knowledge of God. Here, however, two observations
are to be made : Jesus is convinced that he knows
God in a way in which no one ever knew Him
before, and he knows that it is his vocation to
communicate this knowledge of God to others by
word and by deed—and with it the knowledge
that men are God's children. In this consciousness he knows himself to be the Son called and
instituted of God, to be *the* Son of God, and hence
he can say : *My* God and *my* Father, and into
this invocation he puts something which belongs
to no one but himself. How he came to this consciousness of the unique character of his relation to
God as a Son ; how he came to the consciousness
of his power, and to the consciousness of the
obligation and the mission which this power carries
with it, is his secret, and no psychology will
ever fathom it. The confidence with which John
makes him address the Father : "Thou lovedst
me before the foundation of the world" is un-

doubtedly the direct reflection of the certainty
with which Jesus himself spoke. Here all research
must stop. We are not even able to say when
it was that he first knew himself as the Son, and
whether he at once completely identified himself
with this idea and let his individuality be absorbed
in it, or whether it formed an inner problem which
kept him in constant suspense. No one could
fathom this mystery who had not had a parallel
experience. A prophet may, if he chooses, try
to raise the veil, but, for our part, we must be
content with the fact that this Jesus who preached
humility and knowledge of self, nevertheless named
himself and himself alone as *the Son of God*. He
is certain that he knows the Father, that he is
to bring this knowledge to all men, and that
thereby he is doing the work of God. Among
all the works of God this is the greatest; it is
the aim and end of all creation. The work is given
to him to do, and in God's strength he will accomplish it. It was out of this feeling of power
and in the prospect of victory that he uttered the
words: "The Father hath committed all things
unto me." Again and again in the history of
mankind men of God have come forward in the
sure consciousness of possessing a divine message,
and of being compelled, whether they will or not,
to deliver it. But the message has always happened to be imperfect; in this spot or that, defective;
bound up with political or particularistic elements;

designed to meet the circumstances of the moment ;
and very often the prophet did not stand the test
of being himself an example of his message. But
in this case the message brought was of the profoundest and most comprehensive character ; it went
to the very root of mankind and, although set in
the framework of the Jewish nation, it addressed
itself to the whole of humanity — the message
from God the Father. Defective it is not, and its
real kernel may be readily freed from the inevitable husk of contemporary form. Antiquated it
is not, and in life and strength it still triumphs
to-day over all the past. He who delivered it has
as yet yielded his place to no man, and to human
life he still to-day gives a meaning and an aim—
he *the Son of God.*

This already brings us to the other designation
which Jesus gave of himself : *the Messiah.* Before
I attempt briefly to explain it, I ought to mention
that some scholars of note — and among them,
Wellhausen—have expressed a doubt whether Jesus
described himself as the Messiah. In that doubt
I cannot concur ; nay, I think that it is only by
wrenching what the evangelists tell us off its
hinges that the opinion can be maintained. The
very expression " Son of Man "—that Jesus used it
is beyond question—seems to me to be intelligible
only in a Messianic sense. To say nothing of anything else, such a story as that of Christ's entry
into Jerusalem would have to be simply expunged,

if the theory is to be maintained that he did not consider himself the promised Messiah and also desire to be accepted as such. Moreover, the forms in which Jesus expressed what he felt about his own consciousness and his vocation become quite incomprehensible unless they are taken as the outcome of the Messianic idea. Finally, the positive arguments which are advanced in support of the theory are either so very weak, or else so highly questionable, that we may remain quite sure that Jesus called himself the Messiah.

The idea of a Messiah and the Messianic notions generally, as they existed in Jesus' day, had been developed on two combined lines, on the line of the kings and on that of the prophets. Alien influences had also been at work, and the whole idea was transfigured by the ancient expectation that God Himself in visible form would take up the government of His people. The leading features of the Messianic idea were taken from the Israelitish kingdom in the ideal splendour in which it was invested after the kingdom itself had disappeared. Memories of Moses and of the great prophets also played a part in it. In the following lecture we shall briefly show what shapes the Messianic hopes had assumed up to Jesus' time, and in what way he took them up and transformed them.

LECTURE VIII.

ALTHOUGH the Messianic doctrines prevalent in the Jewish nation in Jesus' day were not a positive "dogma," and had no connexion with the legal precepts which were so rigidly cultivated, they formed an essential element of the hopes, religious and political, which the nation entertained for the future. They were of no very definite character, except in certain fundamental features; beyond these the greatest differences prevailed. The old prophets had looked forth to a glorious future in which God would Himself come down, destroy the enemies of Israel, and work justice, peace, and joy. At the same time, however, they had also promised that a wise and mighty king of the house of David would appear and bring this glorious state of things to pass. They had ended by indicating the people of Israel itself as the Son of God, chosen from amongst the nations of the world. These three views exercised a determining influence in the subsequent elaboration of the Messianic ideas. The hope of a glorious future for the people of Israel remained the frame into which all expectations were fitted, but in the two centuries before Christ the following factors were added : (i.) The extension of their historical horizon strengthened the interest of the Jews in the nations of the world, introduced the notion of "mankind" as a whole and brought it within the sphere of the expected end, including, therefore, the operations of the Messiah. The day of judgment is regarded as extending to the whole world, and the Messiah not only as judging the world but as ruling it as well. (ii.) In early times, although the moral purification of the people had been thought of in connexion with the glorious future, the destruction of Israel's enemies seemed to be the main consideration ; but now the feeling of moral responsibility and the knowledge of God as the Holy one became more active ; the view prevails that the Messianic age demands a holy people, and that the judgment to come must of necessity also be a judgment upon a part of Israel itself. (iii) As individualism became a stronger force, so the relation of God to the individual was prominently emphasized. The individual Israelite comes to feel that he is in the midst of his people, and he begins to look upon it as a sum of individuals ; the individual belief in Providence appears side by side with the political belief, and combines with the feeling of personal worth and responsibility ; and in connexion with the expectation of the end, we get the first dawn of the hope of an eternal life and the fear of eternal punishment. The pro-

ducts of this inner development are an interest
in personal salvation, and a belief in the resurrection, and the roused conscience is no longer able
to hope for a glorious future for all in view of
the open profanity of the people and the power
of sin; only a remnant will be saved. (iv.) The
expectations for the future become more and more
transcendent; they are increasingly shifted to the
realm of the supernatural and the supramundane;
something quite new comes down from heaven to
earth, and the new course on which the world enters
severs it from the old; nay, this earth, transfigured
as it will be, is no longer the final goal; the idea
of an absolute bliss arises, whose abode can only
be heaven itself. (v.) The personality of the long-
expected Messiah is sharply distinguished, as well
from the idea of an earthly king, as from the idea
of the people as a whole, and from the idea of
God. Although he appears as a man amongst men,
the Messiah retains scarcely any Messianic traits.
He is represented as with God from the first
beginnings of time; he comes down from heaven,
and accomplishes his work by superhuman means;
the moral traits in the picture formed of him come
into prominence; he is the perfectly just man who
fulfils all the commandments. Nay, the idea that
others benefit by his merits forces its way in.
The notion, however, of a suffering Messiah, which
might seem to be suggested by Isaiah liii., is not
reached.

But none of these speculations succeeded in displacing the older and simpler conceptions, or in banishing that original, patriotic, and political interpretation of them with which the great majority of the people were familiar. God Himself assuming the sceptre, destroying His enemies, founding the Israelitish kingdom of the world, and availing Himself of a kingly champion for the purpose : every man sitting under his own fig-tree, in his own vineyard, enjoying the fruits of peace, with his foot upon the neck of his enemies—that was, after all, still the most popular conception of the coming of the Messiah, and it was fixed in the minds even of those who were at the same time attracted to higher views. But a portion of the people had undoubtedly awakened to the feeling that the kingdom of God presupposes a moral condition of a corresponding character, and that it could come only to a righteous people. Some looked to acquiring this righteousness by means of a punctilious observance of the law, and no zeal that they could show for it was enough ; others, under the influences of a deeper self-knowledge, began to have a dim idea that the righteousness which they so ardently desired could itself come only from the hand of God, and that in order to shake off the burden of sin—for they had begun to be tortured by an inner sense of it—divine assistance, and divine grace and mercy, were needful.

Thus in Christ's time there was a surging chaos of disparate feeling, as well as of contradictory theory, in regard to this one matter. At no other time, perhaps, in the history of religion, and in no other people, were the most extreme antitheses so closely associated under the binding influence of religion. At one moment the horizon seems as narrow as the circle of the hills which surround Jerusalem; at another it embraces all mankind. Here everything is put upon a high plane and regarded from the spiritual and moral point of view ; and there, at but a stone's throw, the whole drama seems as though it must close with a political victory for the nation. In one group all the forces of divine trust and confidence are disengaged, and the upright man struggles through to a solemn "Nevertheless"; in another, every religious impulse is stifled by a morally obtuse, patriotic fanaticism.

The idea which was formed of the Messiah must have been as contradictory as the hopes to which it was meant to respond. Not only were people's formal notions about him continually changing— questions were being raised, for instance, as to the sort of bodily nature which he would have; above all, his inmost character and the work to which he was to be called appeared in diverse lights. But wherever the moral and really religious elements had begun to get the upper hand, people were forced to abandon the image of the political and warlike ruler, and let that of *the prophet*, which had always to some extent helped to form the general notions about the Messiah, take its place. That he would bring God near; that somehow or other he would do justice; that he would deliver from the burden of torment within—this was what was hoped of him. The story of John the Baptist as related in our Gospels makes it clear that there were devout men in the Jewish nation at that time who were expecting a Messiah in this form, or at least did not absolutely reject the idea. We learn from that story that some were disposed to take John for the Messiah. What elasticity the Messianic ideas must have possessed, and how far, in certain circles, they must have travelled from the form which they originally assumed, when this very unkinglike preacher of repentance, clad in a garment of camel's hair, and with no message but that the nation had degenerated and its day of judgment was at hand, could be taken for the Messiah himself. And when the Gospels go on to tell us that not a few among the people took Jesus for the Messiah only because he taught as one with authority, and worked miraculous cures, how fundamentally the idea of the Messiah seems to be changed! They regarded this saving activity, it is true, only as the beginning of his mission; they expected that the wonder-worker would presently throw off his disguise and "set up the kingdom"; but all that we are concerned with here is that they were capable of welcoming as the promised one a man whose origin and previous life they knew, and who had as yet done nothing but preach repentance and proclaim that the kingdom of heaven was at hand. We shall never fathom the inward development by which Jesus passed from the assurance that he was the Son of God to the other assurance that he was the promised Messiah. But when we see that the idea which others as well had formed of the Messiah at that time had, by a slow process of change, developed entirely new features, and had passed from a political and religious idea into a spiritual and religious one—when we see this, the problem no longer wears a character of complete isolation. That John the Baptist and the twelve disciples acknowledged Jesus to be the Messiah; that the positive estimate which they formed of his person did not lead them to reject the shape in which he appeared, but, on the contrary, was fixed in this very shape, is a proof of the flexible character of the Messianic idea at the time, and also explains how it was that Jesus could himself adopt it. "Strength is made perfect in weakness." That there is a divine strength and glory which stands in no need of earthly power and earthly splendour, nay, excludes them; that there is a majesty of holiness and love which saves and blesses those upon whom it lays hold, was what he knew who in spite of his lowliness called himself the Messiah, and the same must have been felt by those who recognised him as the king of Israel anointed of God.

How Jesus arrived at the consciousness of being the Messiah we cannot explain, but still there are some points connected with the question which can be established. An inner event which Jesus experienced at his baptism was in the view of the oldest tradition the foundation of his Messianic consciousness. It is not an experience which is subject to any criticism; still less are we in a position to contradict it. On the contrary, there is a strong probability that when he made his public appearance he had already settled accounts with himself. The evangelists preface their account of his public activity with a curious story of a temptation. This story assumes that he was already conscious of being the Son of God and the one who was intrusted with the all-important work for God's people, and that he had overcome the temptations which this consciousness brought with it. When John sent to him from prison to ask:—" Art thou he that should come, or do we look for another ? " the answer which he sent necessarily led his questioner to understand that he was the Messiah, but at the same time showed him how Jesus conceived the Messianic office. Then came the day at Cæsarea Philippi, when Peter acknowledged him as the expected Messiah, and Jesus joyfully confirmed what he said. This was followed by the question to the Pharisees " What think ye of Christ, whose son is he ? "— the scene which ended with the fresh question: " If David then call him Lord, how is he his son? " Lastly, there was the entry into Jerusalem before the whole people, together with the cleansing of the temple ; actions which were equivalent to a

public declaration that he was the Messiah. But his
first unequivocal Messianic action was also his last.
It was followed by the crown of thorns and the
cross.

I have said that it is probable that when Jesus
made his public appearance he had already settled
accounts with himself, and was therefore clear about
his mission as well. By this, however, I do not
mean that, so far as he himself was concerned,
he had nothing more to learn in the course of
it. Not only had he to learn to suffer, and
to look forward to the cross with confidence in
God, but the consciousness of his Sonship was now
for the first time to be brought to the test. The
knowledge of the "work" which the Father had
intrusted to him could not be developed except by
labour and by victory over all opposition. What
a moment it must have been for him when he
recognised that he was the one of whom the prophets had spoken ; when he saw the whole history
of his nation from Abraham and Moses downwards
in the light of his own mission ; when he could no
longer avoid the conviction that he was the promised
Messiah ! No longer avoid it ; for how can we
refuse to believe that at first he must have felt
this knowledge to be a terrible burden? Yet in
saying this we have gone too far ; and there is
nothing more that we can say. But in this connexion we can understand that the evangelist John
was right in making Jesus testify over and over

again : "I have not spoken of myself; but the Father which sent me ; he gave me a commandment, what I should say, and what I should speak." And again : "For I am not alone, but I and the Father that sent me."

But however we may conceive the "Messiah," it was an assumption that was simply necessary if the man who felt the inward call was to gain an absolute recognition within the lines of Jewish religious history—the profoundest and maturest history that any nation ever possessed, nay, as the future was to show, the true religious history for all mankind. The idea of the Messiah became the means—in the first instance for the devout of his own nation—of effectively setting the man who knew that he was the Son of God, and was doing the work of God, on the throne of history. But when it had accomplished this, its mission was exhausted. Jesus was the "Messiah," and was not the Messiah ; and he was not the Messiah, because he left the idea far behind him ; because he put a meaning into it which was too much for it to bear. Although the idea may strike us as strange we can still feel some of its meaning ; an idea which captivated a whole nation for centuries, and in which it deposited all its ideals, cannot be quite unintelligible. In the prospect of a Messianic period we see once more the old hope of a golden age ; the hope which, when moralised, must necessarily

be the goal of every vigorous movement in human
life and forms an inalienable element in the religious view of history; in the expectation of a
personal Messiah we see an expression of the fact
that it is *persons* who form the saving element in
history, and that if a union of mankind is ever to
come about by their deepest forces and highest aims
being brought into accord, this same mankind
must agree to acknowledge *one* lord and master.
But beyond this there is no other meaning and
no other value to be attached to the Messianic
idea; Jesus himself deprived it of them.

With the recognition of Jesus as the Messiah the
closest possible connexion was established, for every
devout Jew, between Jesus' message and his person;
for it is in the Messiah's activity that God Himself
comes to His people, and the Messiah who does
God's work and sits at the right hand of God in the
clouds of heaven has a right to be worshipped. But
what attitude did Jesus himself take up towards his
Gospel? Does he assume a position in it? To this
question there are two answers; one negative and
one positive.

In those leading features of it which we described
in the earlier lectures the whole of the Gospel is contained, and we must keep it free from the intrusion
of any alien element: God and the soul, the soul and
its God. There was no doubt in Jesus' mind that
God could be found, and had been found, in the law

and the prophets. " He hath showed thee, O Man, what is good ; and what doth the Lord require of thee, but to do justly, and to love mercy, and to walk humbly with thy God." He takes the publican in the temple, the widow and her mite, the lost son, as his examples ; none of them know anything about " Christology," and yet by his humility the publican was justified. These are facts which cannot be turned and twisted without doing violence to the grandeur and simplicity of Jesus' message in one of its most important aspects. To contend that Jesus meant his whole message to be taken provisionally, and everything in it to receive a different interpretation after his death and resurrection, nay, parts of it to be put aside as of no account, is a desperate supposition. No ! his message is simpler than the churches would like to think it ; simpler, but for that very reason sterner and endowed with a greater claim to universality. A man cannot evade it by the subterfuge of saying that as he can make nothing of this " Christology " the message is not for him. Jesus directed men's attention to great questions ; he promised them God's grace and mercy ; he required them to decide whether they would have God or Mammon, an eternal or an earthly life, the soul or the body, humility or self-righteousness, love or selfishness, the truth or a lie. The sphere which these questions occupy is all-embracing ; the individual is called upon to listen to the glad message of mercy and the Fatherhood of God, and to make up his mind whether he will be on God's side and the Eternal's, or on the side of the world and of time. *The Gospel, as Jesus proclaimed it, has to do with the Father only and not with the Son.* This is no paradox, nor, on the other hand, is it "rationalism," but the simple expression of the actual fact as the evangelists give it.

But no one had ever yet known the Father in the way in which Jesus knew Him, and to this knowledge of Him he draws other men's attention, and thereby does "the many" an incomparable service. He leads them to God, not only by what he says, but still more by what he is and does, and ultimately by what he suffers. It was in this sense that he spoke the words, "Come unto me all ye that labour and are heavy laden, and I will give you rest"; as also, "The Son of Man came not to be ministered unto, but to minister and to give his life a ransom for many." He knows that through him a new epoch is beginning, in which, by their knowledge of God, the "least" shall be greater than the greatest of the ages before; he knows that in him thousands—the very individuals who are weary and heavy laden—will find the Father and gain life; he knows that he is the sower who is scattering good seed; his is the field, his the seed, his the fruit. These things involve no dogmatic doctrines; still less any transformation of the Gospel itself, or any oppressive demands upon our faith. They are the expression of an actual fact which he perceives to be already happening, and which, with prophetic assurance, he beholds in advance. When, under the terrible burden of his calling and in the midst of the struggle, he comes to see that it is through him that the blind see, the lame walk, the deaf hear, the poor have the Gospel preached to them, he begins to comprehend the glory which the Father has given him. And he sees that what he now suffers in his person will, through his life crowned in death, remain a fact efficacious and of critical importance for all time : *He is the way to the Father, and as he is the appointed of the Father, so he is the judge as well.*

Was he mistaken ? Neither his immediate posterity, nor the course of subsequent history, has decided against him. It is not as a mere factor that he is connected with the Gospel ; *he was its personal realization and its strength, and this he is felt to be still.* Fire is kindled only by fire ; personal life only by personal forces. Let us rid ourselves of all dogmatic sophistry, and leave others to pass verdicts of exclusion. The Gospel nowhere says that God's mercy is limited to Jesus' mission. But history shows us that he is the one who brings the weary and heavy laden to God ; and, again, that he it was who raised mankind to the new level ; and his teaching is still the touchstone, in that it brings men to bliss and brings them to judgment.

The sentence " I am the Son of God " was not inserted in the Gospel by Jesus himself, and to put that sentence there side by side with the others is

to make an addition to the Gospel. But no one
who accepts the Gospel, and tries to understand him
who gave it to us, can fail to affirm that here the
divine appeared in as pure a form as it can appear
on earth, and to feel that for those who followed
him Jesus was himself the strength of the Gospel.
What they experienced, however, and came to know
in and through him, they have told the world ; and
their message is still a living force.

(6) *The Gospel and doctrine, or the question
of creed.*

We need not dwell long on this question, as on
the essential points—everything that it is necessary to say has already been said in the course of
our previous observations.

The Gospel is no theoretical system of doctrine
or philosophy of the universe ; it is doctrine only
in so far as it proclaims the reality of God the
Father. It is a glad message assuring us of life
eternal, and telling us what the things and
the forces with which we have to do are worth.
By treating of life eternal it teaches us how
to lead our lives aright. It tells us of the
value of the human soul, of humility, of mercy,
of purity, of the cross, and the worthlessness of
worldly goods and anxiety for the things of which
earthly life consists. And it gives the assurance
that in spite of every struggle, peace, certainty,

and something within that can never be destroyed,
will be the crown of a life rightly led. What
else can " the confession of a creed " mean under
these conditions but to do the will of God, in the
certainty that He is the Father and the one who
will recompense? Jesus never spoke of any other
kind of " creed." Even when he says :—" Whosoever shall confess me before men, him will I confess also before my Father which is in Heaven,"
he is thinking of people doing as he did ; he means
the confession which shows itself in feeling and
action. How great a departure from what he thought
and enjoined is involved in putting a " Christological " creed in the forefront of the Gospel, and
in teaching that before a man can approach it he
must learn to think rightly about Christ. That is
putting the cart before the horse. A man can
think and teach rightly about Christ only if, and
in so far as, he has already begun to live according to Christ's Gospel. There is no forecourt to
his message through which a man must pass ; no
yoke which he must first of all take upon himself.
The thoughts and assurances which the Gospel
provides are the first thing and the last thing,
and every soul is directly arraigned before them.

Still less, however, does the Gospel presuppose
any definite knowledge of nature, or stand in any
connexion with such knowledge ; not even in a
negative sense can this contention be maintained.
It is religion and the moral element that are con-

cerned. The Gospel puts the living God before
us. Here, too, the confession of Him in belief
in Him and in the fulfilment of His will is the
sole thing to˙ be confessed; this is what Jesus
Christ meant. So far as the knowledge is concerned—and it is vast—which may be based upon
this belief, it always varies with the measure of
a man's inner development and subjective intelligence. But to possess the Lord of heaven and
earth as a Father is an experience to which nothing else approaches ; and it is an experience which
the poorest soul can have, and to the reality of
which he can bear testimony.

An experience—it is only the religion which a man
has himself experienced that is to be confessed ;
every other creed or confession is in Jesus' view
hypocritical and fatal. If there is no broad " theory
of religion " to be found in the Gospel, still less
is there any direction that a man is to begin by
accepting and confessing any ready-made theory.
Faith and creed are to proceed and grow up out of
the all-important act of turning from the world
and to God, and creed is to be nothing but faith
reduced to practice. " All men have not faith," says
the apostle Paul, but all men ought to be veracious
and be on their guard in religion against lip-ser-
vice and light-hearted assent to creeds. " A certain
man had two sons ; and he came to the first and
said, Son, go work to-day in my vineyard. He
answered and said, I will not ; but afterward he

repented and went. And he came to the second, and said likewise. And he answered and said, I go, Sir; and went not."

I might stop here, but I am impelled to answer one more objection. The Gospel, it is said, is a great and sublime thing, and it has certainly been a saving power in history, but it is indissolubly connected with an antiquated view of the world and history; and, therefore, although it be painful to say so, and we have nothing better to put in its place, it has lost its validity and can have no further significance for us. In view of this objection there are two things which I should like to say :—

Firstly, no doubt it is true that the view of the world and history with which the Gospel is connected is quite different from ours, and that view we cannot recall to life, and would not if we could; but "indissoluble" the connexion is not. I have tried to show what the essential elements in the Gospel are, and these elements are "timeless." Not only are they so; but the man to whom the Gospel addresses itself is also "timeless," that is to say, it is the man who, in spite of all progress and development, never changes in his inmost constitution and in his fundamental relations with the external world. Since that is so, this Gospel remains in force, then, for us too.

Secondly, the Gospel is based—and this is the all-important element in the view which it takes of the world and history—upon the antithesis between Spirit and flesh, God and the world, good and evil. Now, in spite of ardent efforts, thinkers have not yet succeeded in elaborating on a monistic basis any theory of ethics that is satisfactory and answers to the deepest needs of man. Nor will they succeed. In the end, then, it is essentially a matter of indifference what name we give to the opposition with which every man of ethical feeling is concerned: God and the world, the Here and the Beyond, the visible and the invisible, matter and spirit, the life of impulse and the life of freedom, physics and ethics. That there is a unity underlying this opposition is a conviction which can be gained by experience; the one realm can be subordinated to the other; but it is only by a struggle that this unity can be attained, and when it is attained it takes the form of a problem that is infinite and only approximately soluble. It cannot be attained by any refinement of a mechanical process. It is by self-conquest that a man is freed from the tyranny of matter—

Von der Gewalt die alle Wesen bindet
Befreit der Mensch sich der sich überwindet.

This saying of Goethe's excellently expresses the truth that is here in question. It is a truth which holds good for all time, and it forms the essential element in the dramatic pictures of contemporary life in which the Gospel exhibits the antithesis that is to be overcome. I do not know how our increased knowledge of nature is to hinder us from bearing witness to the truth of the creed that "The world passeth away, and the lust thereof, but he that doeth the will of God abideth for ever." We have to do with a dualism which arose we know not how; but as moral beings we are convinced that, as it has been given us in order that we may overcome it in ourselves and bring it to a unity, so also it goes back to an original unity, and will at last find its reconciliation in the great far-off event, the realised dominion of the Good.

Dreams, it may be said; for what we see before our eyes is something very different. No! not dreams—after all it is here that our true life has its root—but patchwork certainly, for we are unable to bring our knowledge in space and time, together with the contents of our inner life, into the unity of a philosophic theory of the world. It is only in the peace of God which passeth all understanding that this unity dawns upon us.

But we have already passed beyond the limits of our immediate task. We proposed to acquaint ourselves with the Gospel in its fundamental features and in its most important bearings. I have tried to respond to this task; but the last point which we touched takes us beyond it. We now return to it, in order to follow, in the second part of these lectures, the course of the Christian religion through history.

LECTURE IX.

THE task before us in the second half of these lectures is to exhibit the history of the Christian religion in its leading phases, and to examine its development in the apostolic age, in Catholicism, and in Protestantism.

THE CHRISTIAN RELIGION IN THE APOSTOLIC AGE.

The inner circle of the disciples, the band of twelve whom Jesus had gathered around him, formed itself into a community. He himself founded no community in the sense of an organised union for divine worship—he was only the teacher and the disciples were the pupils; but the fact that the band of pupils at once underwent this transformation became the ground upon which all subsequent developments rested. What were the characteristic features of this society? Unless I am mistaken there were three factors at work in it: (i.) The recognition of Jesus as the living *Lord*; (ii.) the fact that in every individual member of the new community—including the very slaves—religion was *an*

152

actual experience, and involved the consciousness of a living union with God; (iii.) the leading of *a holy life* in purity and brotherly fellowship, and the expectation of the *Christ's return in the near future.*

By keeping these three factors in view we can grasp the distinctive character of the new community. Let us look at them more closely.

1. *Jesus Christ the Lord:* in thus confessing their belief in him his disciples took the first step in continuing their recognition of him as the authoritative teacher, of his word as their permanent standard of life, of their desire to keep " everything that he commanded them." But this does not express the full meaning attaching to the words " the Lord"; nay, it is far from touching their peculiar significance. The primitive community called Jesus its Lord because he had sacrificed his life for it, and because its members were convinced that he had been raised from the dead and was then sitting on the right hand of God. There is no historical fact more certain than that the apostle Paul was not, as we might perhaps expect, the first to emphasize so prominently the significance of Christ's death and resurrection, but that in recognising their meaning he stood exactly on the same ground as the primitive community. " I delivered unto you first of all," he wrote to the Corinthians, " that which I also received, how that Christ died for our sins according to the Scriptures, and that he was buried, and that he rose again the third day." Paul did, it is true,

make Christ's death and resurrection the subject of
a particular speculative idea, and, so to speak, reduced the whole of the Gospel to these events ;
but they were already accepted as fundamental
facts by the circle of Jesus' personal disciples and
by the primitive community.   In these two facts
it may be said that the permanent recognition of
Jesus Christ, and the reverence and adoration which
he received, obtained their first hold.   They formed
the ground on which the whole Christological theory
rested.   But within two generations from his death
Jesus Christ was already put upon the highest plane
upon which men can put him.   As men were conscious of him as the living Lord, he was glorified as
the one who had been raised to the right hand of God
and had vanquished death, as the Prince of Life,
as the strength of a new existence, as the way,
the truth, and the life.   The Messianic ideas per-
mitted of his being placed upon God's throne,
without endangering monotheism.   But, above all,
he was felt to be the active principle of individual
life : " It is not I that live, but Christ that liveth
in me "; he is " my " life, and to press onwards to
him through death is great gain.   Where can we
find in the history of mankind any similar instance
of men eating and drinking with their master, seeing
him in the characteristic aspects of his humanity,
and then proclaiming him not only as the great
prophet and revealer of God, but as the divine
disposer of history, as the " beginning " of God's

creation, and as the inner strength of a new life! It was not thus that Mahommed's disciples spoke of their prophet. Neither is it sufficient to assert that the Messianic predicates were simply transferred to Jesus, and that everything may be explained by Jesus' expected return in glory throwing its radiance backwards. True, in the certain hope of Jesus' return, his " coming in lowliness " was over-looked; but that it was possible to conceive this certain hope and hold it fast; that in spite of suffering and death it was possible to see in him the promised Messiah; and that in and side by side with the vulgar Messianic image of him, men felt and opened their hearts to him as the present Lord and Saviour, that is what is so astonishing! It was just the death " for our sins," and the resur-rection, which confirmed the impression given by his person, and provided faith with a sure hold: he died as a sacrifice for us and he now lives.

There are many to-day who have come to regard both these positions as very strange; and their at-titude towards them is one of indifference—towards the death, on the ground that no such significance can be attributed to a single event of this kind; to-wards the resurrection, because what is here affirmed to have happened is incredible.

It is not our business to defend either the view which was taken of the death, or the idea that he had risen again; but it is certainly the historian's duty to make himself so fully acquainted with both

positions as to be sensible of the significance which
they possessed and still possess. That these positions
were of capital importance for the primitive community has never been doubted ; even Strauss did
not dispute it ; and the great critic, Ferdinand
Christian Baur, acknowledged that it was on the
belief in them that the earliest Christian communion
was built up. It· must be possible, then, for us in
our turn to get a feeling and an understanding for
what they were ; nay, perhaps we may do more ; if
we probe the history of religion to the bottom, we
shall find the truth and justice of ideas which on the
surface seem so paradoxical and incredible lying at
the very roots of the faith.

Let us first consider the idea that Jesus' death
on the cross was one of expiation. Now, if we were
to consider the conception attaching to the words
" expiatory death" in the alien realm of formal
speculation, we should, it is true, soon find ourselves in a blind alley, and every chance of our
understanding the idea would vanish. We should be
absolutely at the end of our tether if we were to
indulge in speculations as to the necessity which can
have compelled God to require such a sacrificial
death. Let us, in the first place, bear in mind a fact
in the history of religion which is quite universal.
Those who looked upon this death as a sacrifice soon
ceased to offer God any blood-sacrifice at all. The
value attaching to such sacrifices had, it is true,

been in doubt for generations, and had been steadily diminishing; but it was only now that the sacrifices disappeared altogether. They did not disappear immediately or at one stroke—this is a point with which we need not concern ourselves here—but their disappearance took place within a very brief period and was not delayed until after the destruction of the temple. Further, wherever the Christian message subsequently penetrated, the sacrificial altars were deserted and dealers in sacrificial beasts found no more purchasers. If there is one thing that is certain in the history of religion, it is that the death of Christ put an end to all blood-sacrifices. But that they are based on a deep religious idea is proved by the extent to which they existed among so many nations, and they are not to be judged from the point of view of cold and blind rationalism, but from that of vivid emotion. If it is obvious that they respond to a religious need; if, further, it is certain that the instinct which led to them found its satisfaction and therefore its goal in Christ's death; if, lastly, there was the express declaration, as we read in the Epistle to the Hebrews, that " by one offering he hath perfected for ever them that are sanctified," we can no longer feel this idea of Christ's sacrifice to be so very strange; for history has decided in its favour, and we are beginning to get in touch with it. His death had the value of an expiatory sacrifice, for otherwise it would not have had strength to penetrate into that inner world in

which the blood-sacrifices originated; but it was not
a sacrifice in the same sense as the others, or else it
could not have put an end to them; it suppressed
them by settling accounts with them. Nay, we may
go further; the validity of all material sacrifices was
destroyed by Christ's death. Wherever individual
Christians or whole Churches have returned to them,
it has been a relapse : the earliest Christians knew
that the whole sacrificial system was thenceforth
abolished, and if they asked for a reason, they
pointed to Christ's death.

In the second place : any one who will look into
history will find that the sufferings of the pure and
the just are its saving element; that is to say, that
it is not words, but deeds, and not deeds only but
self-sacrificing deeds, and not only self-sacrificing
deeds, but the surrender of life itself, that forms the
turning point in every great advance in history. In
this sense I believe that, however far we may stand
from any *theories* about vicarious sacrifice, there are
few of us after all who will mistake the truth and
inner justice of such a description as we read in
Isaiah liii. : "Surely he hath borne our griefs and
carried our sorrows." "Greater love hath no man
than this, that a man lay down his life for his
friends"—it is in this light that Jesus' death was
regarded from the beginning. Wherever any great
deed has been accomplished in history, the finer a
man's moral feelings are, the more sensible will he be
of vicarious suffering; the more he will bring that

suffering into relation to himself. Did Luther in the monastery strive only for himself?—was it not for us all that he inwardly bled when he fought with the religion that was handed down to him? But it was by the cross of Jesus Christ that mankind gained such an experience of the power of purity and love true to death that they can never forget it, and that it signifies a new epoch in their history.

Finally, in the third place: no reflection of the "reason," no deliberation of the "intelligence," will ever be able to expunge from the moral ideas of mankind the conviction that injustice and sin deserve to be punished, and that everywhere that the just man suffers, an atonement is made which puts us to shame and purifies us. It is a conviction which is inpenetrable, for it comes out of those depths in which we feel ourselves to be a unity, and out of the world which lies behind the world of phenomena. Mocked and denied as though it had long perished, this truth is indestructibly preserved in the moral experience of mankind. These are the ideas which from the beginning onwards have been roused by Christ's death, and have, as it were, played around it. Other ideas have been disengaged—ideas of less importance but, nevertheless, very efficacious at times—but these are the most powerful. They have taken shape in the firm conviction that by his death in suffering he did a definitive work; that he did it "for us." Were we to attempt to measure and register what he did, as was soon attempted, we

should fall into dreadful paradoxes; but we can in
our turn feel it for ourselves with the same freedom
with which it was originally felt.   If we also consider
that Jesus himself described his death as a service
which he was rendering to many, and that by a
solemn act he instituted a lasting remembrance
of it—I see no reason to doubt the fact—we can
understand how this death and the shame of the
cross were bound to take the central place.

Jesus, however, was proclaimed as "the Lord"
not only because he had died for sinners but
because he was the risen and the living one.   If
the resurrection meant nothing but that a deceased
body of flesh and blood came to life again, we
should make short work of this tradition.. But it
is not so. The New Testament itself distinguishes
between the Easter message of the empty grave
and the appearances of Jesus on the one side, and
the Easter faith on the other.   Although the
greatest value is attached to that message, we
are to hold the Easter faith even in its absence.
The story of Thomas is told for the exclusive
purpose of impressing upon us that we must hold
the Easter faith even without the Easter message :
" Blessed are they that have not seen and yet
have believed." The disciples on the road to
Emmaus were blamed for not believing in the
resurrection even though the Easter message had
not yet reached them. The Lord is a Spirit,

says Paul; and this carries with it the certainty of his resurrection. The Easter *message* tells us of that wonderful event in Joseph of Arimathæa's garden, which, however, no eye saw; it tells us of the empty grave into which a few women and disciples looked; of the appearance of the Lord in a transfigured form—so glorified that his own could not immediately recognise him; it soon begins to tell us, too, of what the risen one said and did. The reports became more and more complete, and more and more confident. But the Easter *faith* is the conviction that the crucified one gained a victory over death; that God is just and powerful; that he who is the firstborn among many brethren still lives. Paul based his Easter faith upon the certainty that "the second Adam" was from heaven, and upon his experience, on the way to Damascus, of God revealing His Son to him as still alive. God, he said, revealed him "in me", but this inner revelation was coupled with "a vision" overwhelming as vision never was afterwards. Did the apostle know of the message about the empty grave? While there are theologians of note who doubt it, I think it probable; but we cannot be quite certain about it. Certain it is that what he and the disciples regarded as all-important was not the state in which the grave was found but Christ's appearances. But who of us can maintain that a clear account of these appearances can be constructed out of

the stories told by Paul and the evangelists ; and
if that be impossible, and there is no tradition of
single events which is quite trustworthy, how is
the Easter faith to be based on them ? Either we
must decide to rest our belief on a foundation un-
stable and always exposed to fresh doubts, or else we
must abandon this foundation altogether, and with it
the miraculous appeal to our senses. But here, too,
the images of the faith have their roots in truth
and reality. Whatever may have happened at the
grave and in the matter of the appearances, one
thing is certain : *This grave was the birthplace of
the indestructible belief that death is vanquished,
that there is a life eternal.* It is useless to cite
Plato ; it is useless to point to the Persian religion,
and the ideas and the literature of later Judaism.
All that would have perished and has perished ;
but the certainty of the resurrection and of a life
eternal which is bound up with the grave in
Joseph's garden has not perished, and on the
conviction that *Jesus lives* we still base those
hopes of citizenship in an Eternal City which make
our earthly life worth living and tolerable. " He
delivered them who through fear of death were
all their lifetime subject to bondage," as the writer
of the epistle to the Hebrews confesses. That is
the point. And although there be exceptions to
its sway, wherever, despite all the weight of
nature, there is a strong faith in the infinite value
of the soul ; wherever death has lost its terrors ;

wherever the sufferings of the present are measured against a future of glory, this feeling of life is bound up with the conviction that Jesus Christ has passed through death, that God has awakened him and raised him to life and glory. What else can we believe but that the earliest disciples also found the ultimate foundation of their faith in the living Lord to be the strength which had gone out from him? It was a life never to be destroyed which they felt to be going out from him; only for a brief span of time could his death stagger them; the strength of the Lord prevailed over everything; God did not give him over to death; he lives as the first-fruits of those who have fallen asleep. It is not by any speculative ideas of philosophy but by the vision of Jesus' life and death and by the feeling of his imperishable union with God that mankind, so far as it believes in these things, has attained to that certainty of eternal life for which it was meant, and which it dimly discerns—eternal life in time and beyond time. This feeling first established faith in the value of personal life. But of every attempt to demonstrate the certainty of "immortality" by logical process, we may say in the words of the poet :

Believe and venture : as for pledges,
The Gods give none.

Belief in the living Lord and in a life eternal is the *act* of the freedom which is born of God.

As the crucified and risen one Jesus was the Lord. While this confession of belief in him expressed a man's whole relation to him, it also afforded endless matter for thought and speculation. This conception of the "Lord" came to embrace the many-sided image of the Messiah and all the Old Testament prophecies of a similar kind. But as yet no ecclesiastical "doctrines" about him had been elaborated; everyone who acknowledged him as the Lord belonged to the community.

2. *Religion as an actual experience.* — The second characteristic feature of the primitive community is that every individual in it, even the very slaves, possess a living experience of God. This is sufficiently remarkable; for at first sight we might think that all this devotion to Christ, and this unconditional reverence for him, must necessarily have resulted in all religion becoming a punctilious subjection to his words, and so a kind of voluntary servitude. But the Pauline epistles and the Acts of the Apostles give us quite a different picture. While they do, indeed, attest the fact that Jesus' words were held in unqualified reverence, this fact is not the most prominent feature in the picture of earliest Christendom. What is much more characteristic is that individual Christians, moved by the Spirit of God, are placed in a living and entirely personal relation to God Himself. Dr. Weinel has lately presented us

with a fine work on the "Workings of the Spirit and the Spirits in the post-apostolic age." It contains many passages which take us back to the apostolic age and treat in greater detail of the matters which Professor Gunkel has so impressively placed before us in his treatise on "The Holy Ghost." The neglected problems of the extent to which, and the forms in which, the Spirit exercised an influence on the life of the early Christians, and of the view to be taken of the phenomena connected with this influence, are admirably discussed by Dr. Weinel. In substance, his conclusion is that the expressions "receiving" and "acting by" the Holy Ghost signify such an independence and immediacy of religious life and feeling, and such an inner union with God, perceived to be the mightiest reality, as could not have been expected from strict subjection to Jesus' authority. To be the child of God and to be gifted with the Spirit are simply the same as being a disciple of Christ. That a man is not truly a disciple unless he is pervaded by God's Spirit is a point which the "Acts of the Apostles" fully recognises. The pouring out of the Holy Spirit is placed in the forefront of the narrative. The author is conscious that the Christian religion would not be the highest and the ultimate religion, unless it brought every individual into an immediate and living connexion with God. This mutual union of a full obedient subjection to the

Lord with freedom in the Spirit is the most important feature in the distinctive character of this religion and the seal of its greatness. The workings of the Spirit were shown everywhere, in the entire domain of the five senses, in the sphere of will and action, in profound philosophical speculation, and in the most delicate appreciation of the facts of the moral life. The elementary forces of the religious temperament, long held in check by systems of doctrine and the ceremonies of public worship, were again set free. They showed themselves in ecstatic phenomena, in signs and wonders, in an enhancement of all the functions of life, down to conditions of a pathological and suspicious character. The fact, however, was not forgotten—and where it threatened to be obscured it was strongly impressed on people's attention—that those strange and violent phenomena were individual, but that side by side with them there are workings of the Spirit which are bestowed upon every one and with which no one can dispense. But "The fruit of the Spirit," as the apostle Paul writes, "is love, joy, peace, longsuffering, gentleness, goodness, faith, meekness, temperance." The other feature in the distinctive character and greatness of this religion is that it does not overestimate the elementary strength which gave it birth; that it makes its spiritual purport and its discipline triumph -over all states of ecstacy; and that it holds immoveable to its conviction that the Spirit of God, however it may reveal itself, is a Spirit of holiness and of love. But here we have already passed to the third feature which characterises early Christendom.

3. The third feature is the leading of a *holy life* in purity and brotherly fellowship and in the expectation of Christ's speedy return. The course which the history of the Church followed resulted in the dogmatic details in the New Testament being selected for investigation, rather than those parts of it which depicted the life of the first Christians and exhorted men to morality. And yet not only are the New Testament epistles largely taken up with these moral exhortations, but not a few of the so-called dogmatic portions were also written solely for moral admonition. Jesus directed his disciples to give these exhortations the first place, and the earliest Christians were well aware that the first business of life was to do the will of God and present themselves as a holy community. Upon this their whole existence and their mission in the world were based. There were two points which, in accordance with Jesus' teaching, they put first and foremost, and they were points which at bottom embraced the whole range of moral action : *purity* and *brotherly fellowship*. They took purity in the deepest and most comprehensive sense of the word, as the horror of everything that is unholy, and as the inner pleasure in everything that is upright and true, lovely and of good report. They also meant purity in regard

to the body : " Know ye not that your body is the
temple of the Holy Ghost which is in you ? therefore
glorify God in your body." In this sublime consciousness the earliest Christians took up the struggle
against the sins of impurity, which in the heathen
world were not accounted sins at all. As sons
of God, "blameless and harmless in the midst of a
crooked and perverse nation," they were to "shine as
lights in the world." It was thus that they were
to show of what they were made, and it was thus
that they showed it : to be holy as God was holy,
to be pure as disciples of Christ. Here too, we get
the measure of the renunciation of the world which
this community imposed upon itself. "To keep oneself unspotted from the world" was the asceticism
which it practised itself and required of its adherents. The other point is *brotherly fellowship*. In
joining the love of God with the love of neighbour
in his sayings, Jesus himself had a new union
of men with one another in view. The earliest
Christians understood him. From the very first
they constituted themselves into a brotherly union,
not in word only but in deed—a living realisation
of what he meant. In calling themselves " brothers,"
they felt all the obligations which the name imposes
and tried to come up to them, not by legal regulations but by voluntary service, each according to the
measure of his own powers and gifts. The Acts of
the Apostles tell us that in Jerusalem they went so
far as to have a voluntary community of goods. Paul

says nothing about it ; and if we are to accept this obscure report as really trustworthy, then neither Paul nor the Christian communities among the Gentiles took pattern by the enterprise. They seem not to have been required, nor to have thought it desirable, to order their lives afresh *in externals*. The brotherly fellowship which "the holy" were to cultivate, and did cultivate, was distinguished by two principles : " Whether one member suffer, all the members suffer with it," and " Bear ye one another's burdens and so fulfil the law of Christ."

LECTURE X.

IT was as their Lord that the primitive community of Christians believed in Jesus. They thus expressed their absolute devotion to, and confidence in, him as the Prince of Life. As every individual Christian stood in an immediate relation to God through the Spirit, priests and mediations were no longer wanted. Finally, these "holy" people were drawn together into societies, which bound themselves to a strictly moral life in purity and brotherly fellowship. On the last point let me add a few words.

It is a proof of the inwardness and moral power of the new message that, in spite of the enthusiasm arising from personal experience of religion, there were relatively seldom any extravagant outbursts and violent movements to be combated. Such movements may have been more frequent than the direct declarations of our authorities allow us to suppose, but they did not form the rule; and when they arose Paul was certainly not the only one who was concerned to put them down. He had certainly no wish to quench the "Spirit," but

when enthusiasm threatened to lead to a repug-
nance to work, as in Thessalonica, or when, as in
Corinth, there was a superabundance of ecstatic talk,
he uttered some sober warnings: "If any would
not work, neither should he eat," and "I had
rather speak five words with my understanding,
that by my voice I might teach others also, than
ten thousand words in an unknown tongue." Still
more plainly are the concentrated repose and power
of the leaders shown in the moral admonitions,
such as we get not only in the Pauline Epistles
but also, for example, in the first epistle of Peter
and in the general epistle of James. Christian
character is to show itself in the essential circumstances of human life, and that life is to be
invigorated, supported and illumined by the Spirit.
In the relation of husband to wife and of wife
to husband, of parents to children, of masters
to servants; further, in the individual's relation
to constituted authority, to the surrounding heathen
world, and, again, to the widow and the orphan,
is "the service of God" to be proved and tested.
Where have we another example in history of a
religion intervening with such a robust supernatural consciousness, and at the same time laying
the moral foundations of the earthly life of the
community so firmly as this message? If a man
fails to be inwardly affected by the faith proclaimed
by the New Testament writers, he must certainly
be stirred to the depths by the purity, the wealth,

the power, and the delicacy of the moral knowledge which invests their exhortations with such incomparable value.

There is another feature of the life of the earliest Christians which also deserves notice in this connexion. They lived in the expectation of Christ's near return. This hope supplied them with an extraordinarily strong motive for disregarding earthly things, and the joys and sufferings of this world. That they were mistaken in their expectations we must freely grant; but nevertheless it was a highly efficacious lever for raising them above the world, and teaching them to make little of small things and much of great things, and to distinguish between what is of time and what is of eternity. For a new and powerful religious impulse, which effects its own influence, to be associated with a co-efficient which enhances and strengthens that influence, is what we see constantly happening in the history of religion. With every renewal of the religious experience of sin and grace since Augustine's day, what a lever has been supplied by the *idea of predestination*, and yet it is an idea which is in no way derived from that experience itself. How much enthusiasm was inspired in Cromwell's troops, and how greatly were the Puritans on both sides of the ocean strengthened by *the consciousness of-adoption*, although this consciousness, too, was only a co-efficient. When the religious experiences of St. Francis developed in the Middle

Ages into a new form of devotion, how much assistance it received from the *doctrine of poverty*, and
yet this doctrine was an independent force. The
conviction which obtained in the apostolic age that
the Lord had really appeared after his death on the
cross may also be regarded as a co-efficient. These
co-efficients teach us that the most inward of all
possessions, namely, religion, does not struggle up
into life free and isolated, but grows, so to speak, in
coverings of bark and cannot grow without them.
In studying the apostolic age, however, it is important to observe that, not only in spite of the religious
enthusiasm but even in spite of the intense eschatological hopes which prevailed, the task of making
earthly life holy was not neglected.

The three principles which we have emphasised
as contributing most to the characteristic features
of primitive Christianity could also, if necessary, have
been brought to bear within the framework of
Judaism and in connexion with the synagogue.
There, too, Jesus could have been acknowledged as
the Lord, the new experience united with the
ancestral religion, and the society of brothers developed in the form of a Jewish conventicle. In
Palestine, as a matter of fact, this was the form
which the earliest communities took. But the new
principles displayed great vigour and pointed far
beyond Judaism : Jesus Christ the Lord is not only
Israel's Lord, but the Lord of history, the Lord of

all men. The new experience of a direct union with
God makes the old worship with its priests and
mediations unnecessary. The society of brothers
towers over all other associations and deprives them
of any value. The inner development which the
new tendency virtually comprised began at once.
Paul was not the first to start it; before and side
by side with him there were obscure and nameless
Christians in the dispersion who took up Gentiles
into the new society. They did away with the
particularistic and statutory regulations of the law
by declaring that they were to be understood in a
purely spiritual sense and to be interpreted as
symbols. There was a branch of the Jewish world
outside Palestine where this declaration had long
taken actual effect—it is true, on other grounds—
and where the Jewish religion was being freed from
its limitations by a process of philosophical interpretation which was bringing it to the level of a
spiritual religion for the whole world. This development may be regarded in the light of a preliminary stage in the history of Christianity and
was in many respects really so. It was the stage
on which those nameless Christians entered. It was
the path upon which a deliverance from historical
Judaism and its outworn religious ordinances was
capable of gradual attainment. But one thing is
certain; it was not the goal of the movement. So
long as the words " the former religion is done away
with " remained unspoken, there was always a fear

that in the next generation the old precepts would be brought forward again in their literal meaning. How often and often in the history of religion has there been a tendency to do away with some traditional form of doctrine or ritual which has ceased to satisfy inwardly, but to do away with it by giving it a new interpretation. The endeavour seems to be succeeding; the temper and the knowledge prevailing at the moment are favourable to it —when, lo and behold! the old meaning suddenly comes back again. The actual words of the ritual, of the liturgy, of the official doctrine, prove stronger than anything else. If a new religious idea cannot manage to make a radical breach with the past *at the critical point*—the rest may remain as it is—and procure itself a new "body," it cannot last; it disappears again. There is no tougher or more conservative fabric than a properly constituted religion; it can only yield to a higher phase by being abolished. No permanent effect, then, could be expected in the apostolic age from the twisting and turning of the law so as to make room for the new faith side by side with it, or so as to approximate the old religion to that faith. Someone had to stand up and say " The old is done away with "; he had to brand any further pursuit of it as a *sin*; he had to show that all things were become new. The man who did that was the apostle Paul, and it is in having done it that his greatness in the history of the world consists.

Paul is the most luminous personality in the history of primitive Christianity, and yet opinions differ widely as to his true significance. Only a few years ago we had a leading Protestant theologian asserting that Paul's rabbinical theology led him to corrupt the Christian religion. Others, conversely, have called him the real founder of that religion. But in the opinion of the great majority of those who have studied him the true view is that he was the one who understood the master and continued his work. This opinion is borne out by the facts. Those who blame him for corrupting the Christian religion have never felt a single breath of his spirit, and judge him only by mere externals, such as clothes and book-learning ; those who extol or criticise him as a founder of religion are forced to make him bear witness against himself on the main point, and acknowledge that the consciousness which bore him up and steeled him for his work was illusory and self-deceptive. As we cannot want to be wiser than history, which knows him only as Christ's missionary, and as his own words clearly attest what his aims were and what he was, we regard him as Christ's disciple, as the apostle who not only worked harder but also accomplished more than all the rest put together.

It was Paul who delivered the Christian religion from Judaism. We shall see how he did that if we consider the following points :—

It was Paul who definitely conceived the Gospel as the message of the redemption already effected and of salvation now present. He preached the crucified and risen Christ, who gave us access to God and therewith righteousness and peace.

It was he who confidently regarded the Gospel as a new force abolishing the religion of the law.

It was he who perceived that religion in its new phase pertains to the individual and therefore to all individuals ; and in this conviction, and with a full consciousness of what he was doing, he carried the Gospel to the nations of the world and transferred it from Judaism to the ground occupied by Greece and Rome. Not only are Greeks and Jews to unite on the basis of the Gospel, but the Jewish dispensation itself is now at an end. That the Gospel was transplanted from the East, where in subsequent ages it was never able to thrive properly, to the West, is a fact which we owe to Paul.

It was he who placed the Gospel in the great scheme of spirit and flesh, inner and outer existence, death and life ; he, born a Jew and educated a Pharisee, gave it a *language*, so that it became intelligible, not only to the Greeks but to all *men* generally, and united with the whole of the intellectual capital which had been amassed in previous ages.

These are the factors that go to make the Apostle's greatness in the history of religion. On their inner connexion I cannot here enter in any detail. But, in regard to the first of them, I may remind you of the words of the most important historian

of religion in our day. Wellhausen declares that
" Paul's especial work was to transform the Gospel
of the kingdom into the Gospel of Jesus Christ, so
that the Gospel is no longer the prophecy of the
coming of the kingdom, but its actual fulfilment
by Jesus Christ. In his view, accordingly, redemption from something in the future has become
something which has already happened and is now
present. He lays far more emphasis on faith than
on hope ; he anticipates the sense of future bliss
in the present feeling of being God's son ; he
vanquishes death and already leads the new life on
earth. He extols the strength which is made perfect
in weakness ; the grace of God is sufficient for him,
and he knows that no power, present or future, can
take him from His love, and that all things work
together for good to them that love God." What
knowledge, what confidence, what strength, was
necessary to tear the new religion from its mother
earth and plant it in an entirely new one ! Islam,
originating in Arabia, has remained the Arabian
religion, no matter where it may have penetrated.
Buddhism has at all times been at its purest in India.
But this religion, born in Palestine, and confined by
its founder to Jewish ground, in only a few years
after his death was severed from that connexion.
Paul put it in competition with the Israelitish
religion : " Christ is the end of the law." Not
only did it bear being thus rooted up and transplanted, but it showed that it was meant to be thus

transplanted. It gave stay and support to the Roman empire and the whole world of western civilisation. If, as Renan justly observes, anyone had told the Roman Emperor in the first century that the little Jew who had come from Antioch as a missionary was his best collaborator, and would put the empire upon a stable basis, he would have been regarded as a madman, and yet he would have spoken nothing but the truth. Paul brought new forces to the Roman empire, and laid the foundations of western and Christian civilisation. Alexander the Great's work has perished; Paul's has remained. But if we praise the man who, without being able to appeal to a single word of his master's, ventured upon the boldest enterprise, by the help of the spirit and with the letter against him, we must none the less pay the meed of honour to those personal disciples of Jesus who after a bitter internal struggle ultimately associated themselves with Paul's principles. That Peter did so we know for certain; of others we hear that they at least acknowledged their validity. It was, indeed, no insignificant circumstance that men in whose ears every word of their master's was still ringing, and in whose recollection the concrete features of his personality were still a vivid memory—that these faithful disciples should recognise a pronouncement to be true which in important points seemed to depart from the original message and portended the downfall of the religion of Israel. What was kernel here, and what was husk, history has itself showed with unmistakeable plainness, and by the shortest process. Husk were the whole of the Jewish limitations attaching to Jesus' message ; husk were also such definite statements as " I am not sent but unto the lost sheep of the house of Israel." In the strength of Christ's spirit the disciples broke through these barriers. It was his personal disciples —not, as we might expect, the second or third generation, when the immediate memory of the Lord had already paled—who stood the great test. That is the most remarkable fact of the apostolic age.

Without doing violence to the inner and essential features of the Gospel—unconditional trust in God as the Father of Jesus Christ, confidence in the Lord, forgiveness of sins, certainty of eternal life, purity and brotherly fellowship—Paul transformed it into the universal religion, and laid the ground for the great Church. But whilst the original limitations fell away, new ones of necessity made their appearance ; and they modified the simplicity and the power of a movement which was from within. Before concluding our survey of the apostolic age, we must direct attention to these modifications.

In the first place : the breach with the Synagogue and the founding of entirely independent religious communities had well-marked results. Whilst the idea was firmly maintained that the community of Christ, the " Church," was something suprasensible and heavenly, because it came from within, there was also a conviction that the Church took visible shape in every separate community. As a complete breach had taken place, or no connexion been established, with the ancient communion, the formation of entirely new societies was logically invested with a special significance, and excited the liveliest interest. In his sayings and parables Jesus, careless of all externals, could devote himself solely to the all-important point; but *how and in what forms* the seed would grow was not a question which occupied his mind; he had the people of Israel with their historical ordinances before him and was not thinking of external changes. But the connexion with this people was now severed, and no religious movement can remain in a *bodiless* condition. It must elaborate *forms* for common life and common public worship. Such forms, however, cannot be improvised; some of them take shape slowly out of concrete necessities; others are derived from the environment and from existing circumstances. It was in this way that the "Gentile" communities procured themselves an organism, a body. The forms which they developed were in part independent and gradual, and in part based upon the facts with which they had to deal.

But a special measure of value always attaches to forms. By being the means by which the community is kept together, *the value of that to which they minister is insensibly transferred to them*; or, at least, there is always a danger of this happening. One reason for this is that the observance of the forms can always be controlled or enforced, as the case may be; whilst for the inner life there is no control that cannot be evaded.

When the breach with the Jewish national communion had once taken place, there could be no doubt about the necessity for setting up a new community in opposition to it. The self-consciousness and strength of the Christian movement was displayed in the creation of a Church which knew itself to be the true Israel. But the founding of churches and "the Church" on earth brought an entirely new interest into the field; what came from within was joined by something that came from without; law, discipline, regulations for ritual and doctrine, were developed, and began to assert a position by a logic of their own The measure of value applicable to religion itself no longer remained the only measure, and with a hundred invisible threads religion was insensibly worked into the net of history.

In the second place : we have already referred to the fact that it was above all in his Christology that Paul's significance as a teacher consisted. In his view—we see this as well by the way in which he illuminated the death on the cross and the resurrection, as by his equation, "the Lord is a Spirit"—the Redemption is already accomplished and salvation a present power. "God hath reconciled us to himself through Jesus Christ"; "If any man be in Christ, he is a new creature"; "Who shall separate us from the love of God?"

The absolute character of the Christian religion is thus made clear. But it may also be observed in this connexion that every attempt to formulate a theory has a logic of its own and dangers of its own. There was one danger which the apostle himself had to combat, that of men claiming to be redeemed without giving practical proof of the new life. In the case of Jesus' sayings no such danger could arise, but Paul's formulas were not similarly protected. That men are not to rely upon "redemption," forgiveness of sin, and justification, if the hatred of sin and the imitation of Christ be lacking, inevitably became in subsequent ages a standing theme with all earnest teachers. Who can fail to recognise that the doctrines of "objective redemption" have been the occasion of grievous temptations in the history of the Church, and for whole generations concealed the true meaning of religion? The conception of "redemption," which cannot be inserted in Jesus' teaching in this free and easy way at all, became a snare. No doubt it is true that Christianity is the religion of redemption; but the conception is a delicate one, and must never be taken out of the sphere of personal experience and inner reformation.

But here we are met by a second danger closely connected with the first. If redemption is to be traced to Christ's person and work, everything would seem to depend upon a right understanding of this person together with what he accomplished.

The formation of a correct theory of and about
Christ threatens to assume the position of chief
importance, and to pervert the majesty and simplicity of the Gospel. Here, again, the danger is
of a kind such as cannot arise with Jesus' sayings.
Even in John we read :—" If ye love me, keep
my commandments." But with the way in which
Paul defined the theory of religion, the danger
can certainly arise and did arise. No long period
elapsed before it was taught in the Church that
the all-important thing is to know how the person
of Jesus was constituted, what sort of physical
nature he had, and so on. Paul himself is far
removed from this position—" Whoso calleth Christ
Lord speaketh by the Holy Ghost "—but the way
in which he ordered his religious conceptions, as
the outcome of his speculative ideas, unmistakeably
exercised an influence in a wrong direction. That,
however great the attraction which his way of
ordering them may possess for the understanding,
it is a perverse proceeding to make Christology the
fundamental substance of the Gospel, is shown
by Christ's teaching, which is everywhere directed
to the all-important point, and summarily confronts
every man with his God. This does not affect
Paul's right to epitomise the Gospel in the message
of Christ crucified, thus exhibiting God's power
and God's wisdom, and in the love of Christ
kindling the love of God. There are thousands to-
day in whom the Christian faith is still propagated

in the same manner, namely, through Christ. But to demand assent to a series of propositions about Christ's person is a different thing altogether.

There is, however, another point to be considered here. Under the influence of the Messianic dogmas, and led by the impression which Christ made, Paul became the author of the speculative idea that not only was God in Christ, but that Christ himself was possessed of a peculiar nature of a heavenly kind. With the Jews, this was not a notion that necessarily shattered the framework of the Messianic idea; but with the Greeks it inevitably set an entirely new theory in motion. Christ's *appearance* in itself, the entrance of a divine being into the world, came of necessity to rank as the chief fact, as itself *the real redemption*. Paul did not, indeed, himself look upon it in this light; for him the crucial facts are the death on the cross and the resurrection, and he regards Christ's entrance into the world from an ethical point of view and as an example for us to follow : " For our sakes he became poor "; he humbled himself and renounced the world. But this state of things could not last. The fact of redemption could not permanently occupy the second place ; it was too large. But when moved into the first place it threatened the very existence of the Gospel, by drawing away men's thoughts and interests in another direction. When we look at the history of dogma, who can deny that that was what hap-

pened ?   To what extent it happened we shall
see in the following lectures.

In the third place : the new church possessed a
sacred book, the Old Testament.   Paul, although he
taught that the law had become of no avail, found
a means of preserving the whole of the Old Testament.   What a blessing to the church this book has
proved !   As a book of edification, of consolation, of
wisdom, of counsel, as a book of history, what an
incomparable importance it has had for Christian
life and apologetics !   Which of the religions that
Christianity encountered on Greek or Roman ground
could boast of a similar book ?   Yet the possession of this book has not been an unqualified advantage to the church.   To begin with, there are
many of its pages which exhibit a religion and a
morality other than Christian.   No matter how resolutely people tried to spiritualize it and give it an
inner meaning by construing it in some special way,
their efforts did not avail to get rid of the original
sense in its entirety.   There was always a danger
of an inferior and obsolete principle forcing its way
into Christianity through the Old Testament.   This,
indeed, was what actually occurred.   Nor was it
only in individual aspects that it occurred ; the whole
aim was changed.   Moreover, on the new ground
religion was intimately connected with a political
power, namely, with nationality.   How if people
were seduced into again seeking such a connexion,
not, indeed, with Judaism, but with a new nation,

and not with ancient national laws, but with something of an analogous character? And when even a Paul here and there declared Old Testament laws to be still authoritative in spite of their having undergone an allegorical transformation, how could anyone restrain his successors from also proclaiming other laws, remodelled to suit the circumstances of the time, as valid ordinances of God? This brings us to the second point. Although whatever was drawn from the Old Testament by way of authoritative precept may have been inoffensive in substance, it was a menace to Christian freedom of both kinds. It threatened the freedom which comes from within, and also the freedom to form church communities and to arrange for public worship and discipline.

I have tried to show that the limitations which surrounded the Gospel did not cease with the severance of the tie binding it to Judaism, but that, on the contrary, new limits made their appearance. They arose, however, just at the very points upon which the necessary progress of things depended, or, as the case might be, where an inalienable possession like the Old Testament was in question. Here, again, then, we are reminded of the fact that, so far as history is concerned, as soon as we leave the sphere of pure inwardness, there is no progress, no achievement, no advantage of any sort, that has not its dark side, and does not bring its disadvantages with it. The apostle Paul complained that " we know in part." To a much greater degree is the same thing true of our actions and of everything connected with them. We have always to "pay the penalty" of acting, and not only take the evil consequences but also knowingly and with open eyes resolutely neglect one thing in order to gain another. Our purest and most sacred possessions, when they leave the inward realm and pass into the world of form and circumstance, are no exception to the rule that the very shape which they take in action also proves to be their limitation.

When the great apostle ended his life under Nero's axe in the year 64, he could say of himself what a short time before he had written to a faithful comrade : " I have finished my course; I have kept the faith." What missionary is there, what preacher, what man entrusted with the cure of souls, who can be compared with him, whether in the greatness of the task which he accomplished, or in the holy energy with which he carried it out? He worked with the most living of all messages, and kindled a fire ; he cared for his people like a father and strove for the souls of others with all the forces of his own ; at the same time he discharged the duties of the teacher, the schoolmaster, the organiser. When he sealed his work by his death, the Roman empire from Antioch as far as Rome, nay, as far as Spain, was planted with Christian communities. There were to be found in them few that were " mighty after the flesh" or of noble degree, and yet they were as "lights in the world," and on them the progress of the world's history rested. They had little "illumination," but they had acquired the faith in the living God and in a life eternal; they knew that the value of the human soul is infinite, and that its value is determined by relation to the invisible; they led a life of purity and brotherly fellowship, or at least strove after such a life. Bound together into a new people in Jesus Christ, their head, they were filled with the high consciousness that Jews and Greeks, Greeks and barbarians, would through them become one, and that the last and highest stage in the history of humanity had then been reached.

LECTURE XI.

THE apostolic age now lies behind us. We have seen that in the course of it the Gospel was detached from the mother-soil of Judaism and placed upon the broad field of the Græco-Roman empire. The apostle Paul was the chief agent in accomplishing this work, and in thereby giving Christianity its place in the history of the world. The new connexion which it thus received did not in itself denote any restricted activity; on the contrary, the Christian religion was intended to be realised in mankind, and mankind at that time meant the *orbis Romanus*. But the new connexion involved the development of new forms, and new forms also meant limitation and encumbrance. We shall see more closely how this was effected if we consider

THE CHRISTIAN RELIGION IN ITS DEVELOPMENT INTO CATHOLICISM.

The Gospel did not come into the world as a statutory religion, and therefore none of the forms in which it assumed intellectual and social expression

—not even the earliest—can be regarded as possessing a classical and permanent character. The
historian must always keep this guiding idea before
him when he undertakes to trace the course of the
Christian religion through the centuries from the
apostolic age downwards. As Christianity rises above
all antitheses of the Here and the Beyond, life
and death, work and the shunning of the world,
reason and ecstasy, Hebraism and Hellenism, it
can also exist under the most diverse conditions;
just as it was originally amid the wreck of the
Jewish religion that it developed its power. Not
only can it so exist—it must do so, if it is to be
the religion of the living and is itself to live. As
a Gospel it has only *one* aim—the finding of the
living God, the finding of Him by every individual
as *his* God, and as the source of strength and joy
and peace. How this aim is progressively realised
through the centuries—whether with the co-efficients
of Hebraism or Hellenism, of the shunning of the
world or of civilisation, of Gnosticism or of Agnos-
ticism, of ecclesiastical institution or of perfectly
free union, or by whatever other kinds of bark the
core may be protected, the sap allowed to rise—
is a matter that is of secondary moment, that is
exposed to change, that belongs to the centuries,
that comes with them and with them perishes.

Now the greatest transformation which the new
religion ever experienced—almost greater even than
that which gave rise to the Gentile Church and

thrust the Palestinian communities into the background—falls in the second century of our era, and therefore in the period which we shall consider in the present lecture.

If we place ourselves at about the year 200, about a hundred or a hundred and twenty years after the apostolic age—not more than three or four generations had gone by since that age came to an end—what kind of spectacle does the Christian religion offer?

We see a great ecclesiastical and political community, and side by side with it numerous " sects " calling themselves Christian, but denied the name and bitterly opposed. That great ecclesiastical and political community presents itself as a league of individual communities spanning the Empire from end to end. Although independent they are all constituted essentially alike, and interconnected by one and the same law of doctrine, and by fixed rules for the purposes of intercommunion. The law of doctrine seems at first sight to be of small scope, but all its tenets are of the widest significance; and together they embrace a profusion of metaphysical, cosmological, and historical problems, give them definite answers, and supply particulars of mankind's development from the creation up to its future form of existence. Jesus' injunctions for the conduct of life are not included in this law of doctrine; as the " rule of discipline " they were sharply distinguished from the " rule of faith." Each church, however, also presents itself as an institution for public worship, where God is honoured in conformity with a solemn ritual. The distinction between priests and laymen is already a well-marked characteristic of this institution; certain acts of divine worship can be performed only by the priest; his mediation is an absolute necessity. It is only by mediation that a man can approach God at all, by the mediation of right doctrine, right ordinance, and a sacred book. The living faith seems to be transformed into a creed to be believed; devotion to Christ, into Christology; the ardent hope for the coming of "the kingdom," into a doctrine of immortality and deification; prophecy, into technical exegesis and theological learning; the ministers of the Spirit, into clerics; the brothers, into laymen in a state of tutelage; miracles and miraculous cures disappear altogether, or else are priestly devices; fervent prayers become solemn hymns and litanies; the "Spirit" becomes law and compulsion. At the same time individual Christians are in full touch with the life of the world, and the burning question is, "In how much of this life may I take part without losing my position as a Christian?" This enormous transformation took place within a hundred and twenty years. The first thing which we have to determine is, How did that happen? next, Did the Gospel succeed in holding its own amid this change, and how did it do so?

Before, however, we try to answer these two questions, we must call to mind a piece of advice which no historian ought ever to neglect. Anyone who wants to determine the real value and significance of any great phenomenon or mighty product of history must first and foremost inquire into the work which it accomplished, or, as the case may be, into the problem which it solved. As every individual has a right to be judged, not by this or that virtue or defect, not by his talents or by his frailties, but by what he has done, so the great edifices of history, the States and the Churches, must be estimated first and foremost, we may perhaps say, exclusively, by what they have achieved. It is *the work done* that forms the decisive test. With any other test we are involved in judgments of the vaguest kind, now optimistic, now pessimistic, and mere historical twaddle. So here, too, in considering the church as developed into Catholicism, we must first of all ask, In what did its work consist? What problem did it solve? What did it achieve? I will answer the last question first. It achieved two things: it waged war with nature-worship, polytheism, and political religion, and beat them back with great energy; and it exploded the dualistic philosophy of religion. Had the Church at the beginning of the third century been asked in tones of reproach, "How could you recede so far from where you began? to what have you come?" it might have answered: "Yes, it is to this that I have come; I have been obliged to discard much and admit much; I have had to fight—my body is full of scars, and my clothes are covered with dust; but I have won my battles and built my house; I have beaten back polytheism; I have disabled and almost annihilated that monstrous abortion, political religion; I have resisted the enticements of a subtle religious philosophy, and victoriously encountered it with God the almighty Creator of all things; lastly, I have reared a great building, a fortress with towers and bulwarks, where I guard my treasure and protect the weak." This is the answer which the Church might have given, and truthfully given. But, some one may object, it was no great achievement to wage war with nature-worship and polytheism, and to beat them back; they had already rotted and decayed, and had little strength left. The objection does not hold. Many of the forms in which that species of religion had taken shape were, no doubt, antiquated and approaching extinction, but the religion itself, *the religion of nature*, was a mighty foe. It even still avails to beguile our souls and touch our heart-strings with effect, when an inspired prophet voices its message; how much more so then! The hymn to the Sun, giving life to all that lives, produced a profound and lifelong religious impression even upon a Goethe, and made him into a Sun-worshipper. But how overpowering it was in the days before science had banished the gods from nature. Christianity exploded the religion of nature—exploded it not for this or that individual;

that was already done—but exploded it in the sense that there was now a large and compact community refuting nature-worship and polytheism by its impressive doctrines, and affording the deeper religious temper stay and support. And then political religion! Behind the imperial cult there was the whole power of the state, and to come to terms with it looked so safe and easy—yet the Church did not yield a single inch; it abolished the imperial system of state-idols. It was to place an irremovable landmark between religion and politics, between God and Cæsar, that the martyrs shed their blood. Lastly, in an age that was deeply moved by questions of religious philosophy, the Church maintained a firm front against all the speculative ideas of dualism; and, although these ideas often seemed to approximate closely to its own position, it passionately met them with the monotheistic view. The struggle here, however, was rendered all the harder by the fact that many Christians — and just the very prominent and gifted ones too—made common cause with the enemy, and themselves embraced the dualistic theory. The Church stood firm. If we recollect that, in spite of these counter-movements against the Græco-Roman spirit, it also managed to attach this very spirit to itself—otherwise than Judaism, of whose dealings with the Greek world the saying holds, "You had power to draw but not to keep me"; if we recollect, further, that it was in the second century that the foundations of the whole of the ecclesiastical system prevailing up to the present day were laid, we can only be astonished at the greatness of the work which was then achieved.

We now return to the two questions which we raised : How was this great transformation accomplished? and did the Gospel hold its own amid this change, or, if so, how?

There were, if I am not mistaken, three leading forces engaged in bringing about this great revolution, and effecting the organisation of new forms. The first of these forces tallies with a universal law in the history of religion, for in every religious development we find it at work. When the second and third generations after the founding of a new religion have passed away ; when hundreds, nay thousands, have become its adherents no longer through conversion but by the influences of tradition and of birth—despite Tertullian's saying : *fiunt, non nascuntur Christiani* ; when those who have laid hold upon the faith as great spoil are joined by crowds of others who wrap it round them like an outer garment, a revolution always occurs. The religion of strong feeling and of the heart passes into the religion of custom and therefore of form and of law. A new religion may be instituted with the greatest vigour, the utmost enthusiasm, and a tremendous amount of inner emotion ; it may at the same time lay ever so much stress on spiritual freedom—where was all this ever more powerfully expressed than in Paul's teaching?—and yet, even though believers be forced to be celibates and only adults be received, the process of solidifying and codifying the religion is bound to follow. Its forms then at once stiffen; in the very process of stiffening they receive for the first time a real significance, and new forms are added. Not only do they acquire the value of laws and regulations, but they come to be insensibly regarded as though they contained within them the very substance of religion; nay, as though they were themselves that substance. This is the way in which people who do not feel religion to be a reality are compelled to regard it, for otherwise they would have nothing at all; and this is the way in which those who continue really to live in it are compelled to handle it, or else they would be unable to exercise any influence upon others. The former are not by any means necessarily hypocrites. Real religion, of course, is a closed book to them; its most important element has evaporated. But there are various points of view from which a man may still be able to appreciate religion without living in it. He may appreciate it as discharging the functions of morality, or of police; above all he may appreciate it on æsthetic grounds. When the Romanticists re-introduced Catholicism into Germany and France at the beginning of the nineteenth century, Chateaubriand, more especially, was never tired of singing its praises and fancied that he had all the feelings of a Catholic.

But an acute critic remarked that Monsieur Chateaubriand was mistaken in his feelings; he thought that he was a true Catholic, while as a matter of fact he was only standing before the ancient ruin of the Church and exclaiming: "How beautiful!" That is one of the ways in which a man can appreciate a religion without being an inward adherent of it; but there are many others, and, amongst them, some in which a nearer approach is made to its true substance. All of them, however, have this much in common, that any actual experience of religion is no longer felt, or felt only in an uncertain and intermittent way. Conversely, a high regard is paid to the outward shows and influences connected with it, and they are carefully maintained. Whatever finds expression in doctrines, regulations, ordinances and forms of public worship comes to be treated as the thing itself. This, then, is the first force at work in the transformation : *the original enthusiasm*, in the large sense of the word, *evaporates*, and the religion of law and form at once arises.

But not only did an original element evaporate in the course of the second century; another was introduced. Even had this youthful religion not severed the tie which bound it to Judaism, it would have been inevitably affected by the spirit and the civilisation of that Græco-Roman world on whose soil it was permanently settled. But to what a much greater extent was it exposed to the influence of this spirit after being sharply severed from the

Jewish religion and the Jewish nation. It hovered bodiless over the earth like a being of the air ; bodiless and seeking a body. The spirit, no doubt, makes to itself its own body, but it does so by assimilating what is around it. The influx of Hellenism, of the Greek spirit, and the union of the Gospel with it, form the greatest fact in the history of the Church in the second century, and when the fact was once established as a foundation it continued through the following centuries. In the influence of Hellenism on the Christian religion three stages may be distinguished, and a preliminary stage as well. We have already mentioned the preliminary stage in a previous lecture. It is to be found in the circumstances in which the Gospel arose, and it formed a very condition of its appearance. Not until Alexander the Great had created an entirely new position of affairs, and the barriers separating the nations of the East from one another and from Hellenism had been destroyed, could Judaism free itself from its limitations and start upon its development into a religion for the world. The time was ripe when a man in the East could also breathe the air of Greece and see his spiritual horizon stretch beyond the limits of his own nation. Yet we cannot say that the earliest Christian writings, let alone the Gospel, show, to any considerable extent, the presence of a Greek element. If we are to look for it any-where—apart from certain well-marked traces of it in Paul, Luke, and John—it must be in the *possi-*

bility of the new religion appearing at all. We cannot enter further upon this question here. The first stage of any real influx of definitely Greek thought and Greek life is to be fixed at about the year 130. It was then that the religious philosophy of Greece began to effect an entrance, and it went straight to the centre of the new religion. It sought to get into inner touch with Christianity, and, conversely, Christianity itself held out a hand to this ally. We are speaking of Greek *philosophy* ; as yet, there is no trace of mythology, Greek worship, and so on ; all that was taken up into the Church, cautiously and under proper guarantees, was the great capital which philosophy had amassed since the days of Socrates. A century or so later, about the year 220 or 230, the second stage begins : Greek mysteries, and Greek civilisation in the whole range of its development, exercise their influence on the Church, but not mythology and polytheism ; these were still to come. Another century, however, had in its turn to elapse before Hellenism as a whole and in every phase of its development was established in the Church. Guarantees, of course, are not lacking here either, but for the most part they consist only in a change of label ; the thing itself is taken over without alteration, and in the worship of the saints we see a regular Christian religion of a lower order arising. We are here concerned, however, not with the second and third stage, but only with that influx of the Greek spirit which was marked by the absorption of Greek philosophy and, particularly, of Platonism. Who can deny that elements here came together which stood in elective affinity? So much depth and delicacy of feeling, so much earnestness and dignity, and—above all—so strong a *monotheistic* piety were displayed in the religious ethics of the Greeks, acquired as it had been by hard toil on a basis of inner experience and metaphysical speculation, that the Christian religion could not pass this treasure by with indifference. There was much in it, indeed, which was defective and repellent; there was no personality visibly embodying its ethics as a living power; it still kept up a strange connexion with "demon-worship" and polytheism; but both as a whole and in its individual parts it was felt to contain a kindred element, and it was absorbed.

But besides the Greek ethics there was also a cosmological conception which the Church took over at this time, and which was destined in a few decades to attain a commanding position in its doctrinal system—*the Logos.* Starting from an examination of the world and the life within, Greek thought had arrived at the conception of an *active central idea*—by what stages we need not here mention. This central idea represented the unity of the supreme principle of the world, of thought, and of ethics; but it also represented, at the same time, the divinity itself as a creative and active as distinguished from a quiescent power. The most important step that was ever taken in the domain of Christian doctrine was when the Christian apologists at the beginning of the second century drew the equation : the Logos = Jesus Christ. Ancient teachers before them had also called Christ " the Logos " among the many predicates which they ascribed to him ; nay, one of them, John, had already formulated the proposition : " The Logos is Jesus Christ." But with John this proposition had not become the basis of every speculative idea about Christ ; with him, too, " the Logos " was only a predicate. But now teachers came forward who previous to their conversion had been adherents of the platonico-stoical philosophy, and with whom the conception " Logos " formed an inalienable part of a general philosophy of the world. They proclaimed that Jesus Christ was the Logos incarnate, which had hitherto been revealed only in the great effects which it exercised. In the place of the entirely unintelligible conception " Messiah," an intelligible one was acquired at a stroke ; Christology, tottering under the exuberance of its own affirmations, received a stable basis ; Christ's significance for the world was established ; his mysterious relation to God was explained ; the cosmos, reason, and ethics, were comprehended as one. It was, indeed, a marvellous formula ; and was not the way prepared for it, nay hastened, by the speculative ideas about the Messiah propounded by Paul and other ancient teachers ? The knowledge that the divine in Christ must be conceived as the Logos opened up a number

of problems, and at the same time set them definite
limits and gave them definite directives. Christ's
unique character as opposed to all rivals appeared
to be established in the simplest fashion, and yet
the conception provided thought with so much
liberty and free play that Christ could be regarded,
as the need might arise, on the one side as operative
deity itself, and on the other as still the first
born among many brethren and as the first created
of God.

What a proof it is of the impression which Christ's
teaching created that Greek philosophers managed
to identify him with the Logos! For the assertion
that the incarnation of the Logos had taken place
in an historical personage there had been no pre-
paration. No philosophising Jew had ever thought
of identifying the Messiah with the Logos; no
Philo, for instance, ever entertained the idea of
such an equation! *It gave a metaphysical significance to an historical fact; it drew into the domain
of cosmology and religious philosophy a person
who had appeared in time and space;* but by so
distinguishing one person it raised all history to
the plane of the cosmical movement.

The identification of the Logos with Christ was the
determining factor in the fusion of Greek philosophy
with the apostolic inheritance and led the more
thoughtful Greeks to adopt the latter. Most of us
regard this identification as inadmissible, because the
way in which we conceive the world and ethics does

not point to the existence of any logos at all. But a man must be blind not to see that for that age the appropriate formula for uniting the Christian religion with Greek thought was the Logos. Nor is it difficult even to-day to attach a valid meaning to the conception. An unmixed blessing it has not been. To a much larger extent than the earlier speculative ideas about Christ it absorbed men's interest; it withdrew their minds from the simplicity of the Gospel, and increasingly transformed it into a philosophy of religion. The proposition that the Logos had appeared among men had an intoxicating effect, but the enthusiasm and transport which it produced in the soul did not lead with any certainty to the God whom Jesus Christ proclaimed.

The loss of an original element and the gain of a fresh one, namely, the Greek, are insufficient to explain the great change which the Christian religion experienced in the second century. We must bear in mind, thirdly, the great struggle which that religion was then carrying on within its own domain. Parallel with the slow influx of the element of Greek philosophy experiments were being made all along the line in the direction of what may be briefly called "acute Hellenisation." While they offer us a most magnificent historical spectacle, in the period itself they were a terrible danger. More than any before it, the second century is the century of religious fusion, of theocracy. The problem was to bring Christianity into the realm of theocracy, as

one element among others, although the chief. The
"Hellenism" which made this endeavour had already
attracted to itself all the mysteries, all the philosophy
of Eastern worship, elements the most sublime and
the most absurd, and by the never failing aid of
philosophical, that is to say, of allegorical interpretation, had spun them all into a glittering web. It
now fell upon—I cannot help so expressing it—the
Christian religion. It was impressed by the sublime
character of this religion; it did reverence to Jesus
Christ as the Saviour of the world; it offered to
give up everything that it possessed—all the treasures
of its civilisation and its wisdom—to this message, if
only the message would suffer them to stand. As
though endowed with the right to rule, the message
was to make its entry into a ready-made theory of
the world and religion, and into mysteries already
prepared for it. What a proof of the impression
which this message made, and what a temptation!
This "Gnosticism"—such is the name which the
movement has received—strong and active in the
plenitude of its religious experiments, established
itself under Christ's name, developed a vigorous and
abiding feeling for many Christian ideas, sought to
give shape to what was still shapeless, to settle
accounts with what was externally incomplete, and
to bring the whole stream of the Christian movement
into its own channel. The majority of the faithful,
led by their bishops, so far from yielding to these
enticements, took up the struggle with them in the

conviction that they masked a demonic temptation. But struggle in this case meant definition, that is to say, drawing a sharp line of demarcation around what was Christian and declaring everything heathen that would not keep within it. *The struggle with Gnosticism compelled the Church to put its teaching, its worship, and its discipline, into fixed forms and ordinances, and to exclude everyone who would not yield them obedience.* In the conviction that it was everywhere only conserving and honouring what had been handed down, it never for a moment doubted that the obedience which it demanded was anything more than subjection to the divine will itself, and that in the doctrines with which it encountered the enemy it was exhibiting *the impress of religion itself.*

If by "Catholic" we mean the church of doctrine and of law, then the Catholic church had its origin in the struggle with Gnosticism. It had to pay a heavy price for the victory which kept that tendency at bay; we may almost say that the vanquished imposed their terms upon the victor: *Victi victoribus legem dederunt.* It kept Dualism and the acute phase of Hellenism at bay; but by becoming a community with a fully worked out scheme of doctrine, and a definite form of public worship, it was of necessity compelled to take on forms analogous to those which it combated in the Gnostics. To encounter our enemy's theses by setting up others one by one, is to change over to his ground. How much of its original freedom the Church sacrificed! It was now forced to say : You are no Christian, you cannot come into any relation with God at all, unless you have first of all acknowledged these doctrines, yielded obedience to these ordinances, and followed out definite forms of mediation. Nor was anyone to think a religious experience legitimate that had not been sanctioned by sound doctrine and approved by the priests. The Church found no other way and no other means of maintaining itself against Gnosticism, and what was set up as a protection against enemies from without became the palladium, nay, the very foundation, within. This entire development, it is true, would probably have taken place apart from the struggle in question—the two elements which we first discussed would have produced it— but that it took place so rapidly and assumed so positive, nay, so Draconian, a shape, was due to the fact that the struggle was one in which the very existence of the traditional religion was at stake. The superficial view that the personal ambition of certain individuals was at the bottom of the whole system of established ordinance and priesthood is absolutely untenable. The loss of the original, living element is by itself sufficient to explain the phenomena. *La médiocrité fonde l'autorité.* It is the man who knows religion only as usage and obedience that creates the priest, for the purpose of ridding himself of an essential part of the obligations which he feels by loading him with them.   He also makes ordinances, for the semi-religious prefer an ordinance to a Gospel.

We have endeavoured to indicate the tendencies by which the great change was effected.   It remains to answer the second question : Did the Gospel hold its own amid the change, and, if so, how ?   That it entered upon an entirely new set of circumstances is already obvious ; but we shall have to study them more closely.

LECTURE XII.

No one can compare the internal state of Christendom at the beginning of the third century with the state in which it found itself a hundred and twenty years earlier without being moved by conflicting views and sentiments. Admiration for the vigorous achievement presented in the creation of the Catholic Church, and for the energy with which it extended its activity in all directions, is balanced by concern at the absence of those many elements of freedom and directness, united, however, by an inward bond, which the primitive age possessed. Although we are compelled gratefully to acknowledge that this Church repelled all attempts to let the Christian religion simply dissolve into contemporary thought, and protected itself against the acute phase of Hellenisation, still we cannot shut our eyes to the fact that it had to pay a high price for maintaining its position. Let us determine a little more precisely what the alteration was which was effected in it, and on which we have already touched.

The first and most prominent change is the way in which freedom and independence in matters of religion is endangered. No one is to feel and count himself a Christian, that is to say, a child of God, who has not previously subjected his religious knowledge and experience to the controlling influence of the Church's creed. The "Spirit" is confined within the narrowest limits, and forbidden to work where and as it will. Nay, more; not only is the individual, except in special cases, to begin by being a minor and by obeying the Church; he is never to become of full age, that is to say, he is never to lose his dependence on doctrine, on the priest, on public worship, and on the "book." It was then that what we still specifically call the Catholic form of godliness, in contrast with Evangelicalism, originated. A blow was dealt to the direct and immediate element in religion; and for any individual to restore it afresh for himself became a matter of extraordinary difficulty.

Secondly, although the acute phase of Hellenisation was avoided, Christendom became more and more penetrated by the Greek and philosophical idea that true religion is first and foremost "doctrine," and doctrine, too, that is coextensive with the whole range of knowledge. That this faith of "slaves and old women" attracted to itself the entire philosophy of God and the world which the Greeks had formed, and undertook to recast that philosophy as though teaching it were part of its own substance, and unite it with the teaching of Jesus Christ, was certainly a proof of the inner power of the Christian

212 WHAT IS CHRISTIANITY?

religion; but the process involved, as a necessary
consequence, a displacement of the fundamental
religious interest, and the addition of an enormous
burden. The question "What must I do to be
saved?" which in Jesus Christ's and the Apostles'
day could still receive a very brief answer, now
evoked a most diffuse one; and even though in view
of the laymen shorter replies might still be provided,
the laymen were in so far regarded as imperfect, and
expected to observe a submissive attitude towards the
learned. The Christian religion had already received
that tendency to Intellectualism which has clung
to it ever since. But when thus presented as a
huge and complex fabric, as a vast and difficult
system of doctrine, not only is it encumbered, but
its earnest character threatens to disappear. This
character depends upon the emotional and gladdening
element in it being kept directly accessible. The
Christian religion is assuredly informed with the desire
to come to terms with all knowledge and with intellectual life as a whole; but when achievements in
this field—even presuming that they always accord
with truth and reality—are held to be equally binding
with the evangelical message, or even to be a necessary preliminary to it, mischief is done to the cause
of religion. This mischief is already unmistakeably
present at the beginning of the third century.

Thirdly, the church obtained a special, independent value as an *institution*; it became a *religious
power*. Originally only a developed form of that

community of brothers which furnished place and
manner for God's common worship and a mysterious shadow of the heavenly Church, it now
became, *as an institution*, an indispensable factor
in religion. People were taught that in this institution Christ's Spirit had deposited everything that
the individual man can need; that he is wholly
bound to it, therefore, not only in love but also in
faith; that it is there only that the Spirit works,
and therefore there only that all its gifts of grace
are to be found. That the individual Christian
who did not subordinate himself to the ecclesiastical institution relapsed, as a rule, into heathenism,
and fell into false and evil doctrines or an immoral
life, was, indeed, an actual fact. The effect of this,
combined with the struggle against the Gnostics, was
that the institution, together with all its forms and
arrangements, became more and more identified with
the "bride of Christ," "the true Jerusalem," and so
on, and accordingly was even itself proclaimed as
the inviolable creation of God, and the fixed and
unalterable abode of the Holy Ghost. Consistently
with this, it began to announce that all its ordinances
were equally sacred. How greatly religious liberty
was thus encumbered I need not show.

Fourthly and lastly, the Gospel was not proclaimed as the glad message with the same vigour
in the second century as it had been in the first.
The reasons for this are manfold : on the one hand
personal experience of religion was not felt so

strongly as Paul, or as the author of the fourth
gospel, felt it; on the other, the prevalent eschatological expectations, which those teachers had re-
strained by their more profound teaching, remained
in full sway. *Fear* and *hope* are more prominent in
the Christianity of the second century than they are
with Paul, and it is only in appearance that the
former stands nearer to Jesus' sayings; for, as we
saw, God's Fatherhood is the main article in Jesus'
message.   But, as Romans viii. proves, the knowledge of this truth is just what Paul embodied in
his preaching of the faith.   While the element of
fear thus obtained a larger scope in the Christianity of the second century—this scope increased
in proportion as the original buoyancy died down
and conformity to the world extended—the ethical
element became less free and more a matter of law
and rigorism.   In religion, rigorism always forms
the obverse side of secularity.   But as it appeared
impossible to expect a rigoristic ethics of everyone, the distinction between a perfect and a sufficient morality already set in as an element in the
growth of Catholicism.   That the roots of this
distinction go further back is a fact of which we
need not here take account; it was only towards
the end of the second century that the distinction became a fatal one.   Born of necessity and
erected into a virtue, it soon grew so important
that the existence of Christianity as a Catholic
Church came to depend upon it.   The uniformity of

the Christian ideal was thereby disturbed and a quantitative view of moral achievement suggested which is unknown to the Gospel. The Gospel does, no doubt, make a distinction between a strong and a weak faith, and greater and smaller moral achievements; but he that is least in the kingdom of God may be perfect in his kind.

These various tendencies together denote the essential changes which the Christian religion experienced up to the beginning of the third century, and by which it was modified. Did the Gospel hold its own in spite of them, and how may that be shown? Well, we can cite a whole series of documents, which, so far as written words can attest inner and genuinely Christian life, bear very clear and impressive testimony that such life existed. Martyrdoms like those of Perpetua and Felicitas, or letters passing between communities, like those from Lyons to Asia Minor, exhibit the Christian faith and the strength and delicacy of moral sentiment with a splendour only paralleled in the days when the faith was founded; while of all that had been done in the external development of the Church they make no mention whatever. The way to God is found with certainty, and the simplicity of the life within does not appear to be disturbed or encumbered. Again, let us take a writer like the Christian religious philosopher, Clement of Alexandria, who flourished about the year 200. We can still feel from his writings that this scholar, although he was absolutely steeped in speculative ideas, and as a thinker reduced the Christian religion to a boundless sea of " doctrines "—a Greek in every fibre of his being —won peace and joy from the Gospel, and he can also express what he won and testify of the power of the living God. It is as a new man that he appears, one who has pressed on through the whole range of philosophy, through authority and speculation, through all the externals of religion, to the glorious liberty of the children of God. His faith in Providence, his faith in Christ, his doctrine of freedom, his ethics — everything is expressed in language that betrays the Greek, and yet everything is new and genuinely Christian. Further, if we compare him with a Christian of quite another stamp, namely, his contemporary Tertullian, it is easy to show that what they have in common in religion is what they have learned from the Gospel, nay, is the Gospel itself. And in reading Tertullian's exposition of the Lord's Prayer and turning it over in our minds, we see that this hot-blooded African, this stern foe of heretics, this resolute champion of *auctoritas* and *ratio*, this dogmatic advocate, this man, at once Churchman and enthusiast, nevertheless possessed a deep feeling for the main substance of the Gospel and a good knowledge of it as well. In this Old-Catholic Church the Gospel, truly, was not as yet stifled !

Further, this Church still kept up the all-important idea that the Christian community must present itself as a society of brothers active in work, and it gave expression to this idea in a way that puts subsequent generations to shame.

Lastly, there can be no doubt—and while so truth-loving a man as Origen confirms the fact for us, heathen writers like Lucian also attest it—that the hope of an eternal life, the full confidence in Christ, a readiness to make sacrifices, and a purity of morals, were still, in spite of all frailties—here, too, not lacking—the *real* characteristics of this society. Origen can challenge his heathen opponents to compare any community whatever with the Christian community, and to say where the greater moral excellence lies. This religion had, no doubt, already developed a husk and integument, to penetrate through to it and grasp the kernel had become more difficult; it had also lost much of its original life. But the gifts and the tasks which the Gospel offered still remained in force, and the fabric which the Church had erected around them also served many a man as the means by which he attained to the thing itself.

We now pass to the consideration of

THE CHRISTIAN RELIGION IN GREEK CATHOLICISM.

I must invite you to descend several centuries with me and to look at *the Greek Church* as it

is to-day, and as it has been preserved, essentially
unaltered, for more than a thousand years. Between
the third and the nineteenth century the history
of the Church of the East nowhere presents any
deep gulf. Hence we may take up our position
in the present. Here, in turn, we ask the three
following questions :—

What did this Greek Catholicism achieve?

What are its characteristics?

What modifications did the Gospel here undergo
and how did it hold its own?

What did this Greek Catholicism achieve?
Two facts may be cited on this point : firstly, in
the great domain which it embraces, the countries
of the eastern part of the Mediterranean and north-
wards to the Arctic Ocean, it made an end of
heathenism and polytheism. The decisive victory
was accomplished from the third to the sixth
century, and so effectually accomplished that the
gods of Greece really perished—perished unwept
and unmourned. Not in any great battle did they
die, but from sheer exhaustion, and without offering
any resistance worth mention. I may just point
out that before dying they transferred a considerable
portion of their power to the Church's saints. But
what is more important, with the death of the gods,
Neoplatonism, the last great product of Greek
philosophy, was also vanquished. The religious
philosophy of the Church proved the stronger. The
victory over Hellenism is an achievement of the

Eastern Church on which it still subsists. Secondly, this Church managed to effect such a fusion with the individual nations which it drew into its bosom that religion and church became to them national palladia, nay, palladia pure and simple. Go amongst Greeks, Russians, Armenians, etc., and you will everywhere find that religion and nationality are inseparable, and the one element exists only in and alongside of the other. Men of these nationalities will, if need be, suffer themselves be cut in pieces for their religion. This is no mere consequence of the pressure exercised by the hostile power of Mohammedanism; the Russians are not subject to this pressure. Nor is it only — shall I say ? — in the Moscow press that we can see what a firm and intimate connexion exists between Church and nation in these peoples, in spite of "sects" which are not wanting here either; to convince ourselves of it we must read—to take an instance at random—Tolstoi's *Village Tales*. They bring before the reader a really touching picture of the deep influence of the Church, with its message of the Eternal, of self-sacrifice, of sympathy and fraternity, on the national mind. That the clergy stand low in the social scale, and frequently encounter contempt, must not delude us into supposing that as the representatives of the Church they do not occupy an incomparably high station. In Eastern Europe the monastic ideal is deeply rooted in the national soul.

But the mention of these two points includes everything that can be said about the achievements of this Church. To add that it has disseminated a certain amount of culture would involve pitching our standard of culture very low. In comparison with Islam, too, it is no longer so successful in doing what it has done in the past and still does in regard to polytheism. The missions of the Russian Church are still overthrowing polytheism even to-day; but large territories have been lost to Islam, and the Church has not recovered them. Islam has extended its victories as far as the Adriatic and in the direction of Bosnia. It has won over numerous Albanian and Slav tribes which were once Christian. It shows itself to be at least a match for the Church, although we must not forget that in the heart of its dominions there are Christian nations who have maintained their creed.

Our second question was, What are the characteristics of this Church? The answer is not easy; for as it presents itself to the spectator this Church is a highly complex structure. The feelings, the superstitions, the learning, and the devotional philosophy of hundreds, nay, of thousands of years, are built into it. But, further; no one can look at this Church from outside, with its forms of worship, its solemn ritual, the number of its ceremonies, its relics, pictures, priests, monks, and the philosophy of its mysteries, and then compare it on the one hand with the Church of the first century, and on the other with the Hellenic cults in the age of Neoplatonism, without arriving at the conclusion that it belongs not to the former but to the latter. *It takes the form, not of a Christian product in Greek dress, but of a Greek product in Christian dress.* It would have done battle with the Christians of the first century just as it did battle with the worship of Magna Mater and Zeus Soter. There are innumerable features of this Church which are counted as sacred as the Gospel, and towards which not even a tendency existed in primitive Christianity. Of the whole performance of the chief religious service, nay, even of many of the dogmas, the same thing may, in the last resort, be said : if certain words, like Christ, etc., are omitted, there is nothing left to recall the original element. In its external form as a whole this Church is nothing more than a continuation of the history of Greek religion under the alien influence of Christianity, parallel to the many other alien influences which have affected it. We might also describe it as the natural product of the union between Hellenism, itself already in a state of oriental decay, and Christian teaching; it is the transformation which history effects in a religion by "natural" means, and, as was here the case, was bound to effect between the third and the sixth century. In this sense it is *a natural religion.* The conception admits of a double meaning. It is generally understood as an abstract

term covering all the elementary feelings and pro-
cesses traceable in every religion. Whether there are
any such elements, or, on the other hand, whether
they are sufficiently stable and articulate to be
followed as a whole, admits, however, of a doubt.
The conception "natural religion" may be better
applied to the growth which a religion produces when
the "natural" forces of history have ceased playing on
it. At bottom these forces are everywhere the same,
although differing in the way in which they are
mounted. They mould religion until it answers
their purpose ; not by expelling what is sacred,
venerable, and so on, but by assigning it the
place and allowing it the scope which they consider
right. They immerse everything in a uniform
medium,—that medium which, like the air, is the
first condition of their "natural" existence. In
this sense, then, the Greek Church is a *natural*
religion ; no prophet, no reformer, no genius, has
arisen in its history since the third century to
disturb the ordinary process by which a religion
becomes naturalised into common history. The
process attained its completion in the sixth century
and asserted itself victoriously against severe assaults
in the eighth and ninth. The Church has since been
at rest, and no further essential, nay, not even any
unessential, change has taken place in the condition
which it then reached. Since then, apparently, the
nations belonging to this Church have undergone
nothing to make it seem intolerable to them and

to call for any reform in it. They still continue, then, in this "natural" religion of the sixth century.

I have, however, advisedly spoken of the Church in its external form. Its complex character is partly due to the fact that we cannot arrive at its inner condition by simple deduction from its outer. It is not sufficient to observe, although the observation is correct, that this Church is part of the history of Greek religion. It exercises influences which from this point of view are not easily intelligible. We cannot form a correct estimate of it unless we dwell more closely on the factors which lend it its character.

The first factor which we encounter is *tradition*, and the observance of it. The sacred and the divine do not exist in free action—we shall see later to what reservations this statement is subject—but are put, as it were, into a storehouse, in the form of an immense capital. The capital is to provide for all demands, and to be coined in the precise way in which the Fathers coined it. Here, it is true, we have an idea which can be traced to something already existing in the primitive age. We read in the Acts of the Apostles that "They continued steadfastly in the apostles' doctrine." But what became of this practice and this obligation? Firstly, everything was designated "apostolic" which was deposited in this Church in the course of the succeeding centuries; or, rather, what the Church considered necessary to possess in order to suit the historical position in which it was placed, it called apostolic, because it fancied that otherwise it could not exist, and what is necessary for the Church's existence *must* be simply apostolic. Secondly, it has been established as an irrefragable fact that the "continuing steadfastly in the apostles' doctrine" applies, first and foremost, to the punctilious observance of every direction as to ritual: the sacred element is bound up with *text* and *form*. Both are conceived in a thoroughly antique way. That the divine is, so to speak, stored up as though it were an actual commodity, and that the supreme demand which the Deity makes is the punctilious observance of a ritual, were ideas that in antiquity were perfectly familiar and admitted of no doubt. Tradition and ceremony are the conditions under which the Holy alone existed and was accessible. Obedience, respect, reverence, were the most important religious feelings. Whilst they are doubtless inalienable features of religion, it is only as accompaniments of an active feeling quite different in its character that they possess any value, and that further presumes that the object to which they are directed is a worthy one. Traditionalism and the ritualism so closely connected with it are prominent.characteristics of the Greek Church, but this is just what shows how far it has departed from the Gospel.

The second point that fixes the character of this Church is the value which it attaches to *orthodoxy*, to sound doctrine. It has stated and re-stated its doctrines with the greatest precision and often enough made them a terror to men of different creed. No one, it claims, can be saved who does not possess the correct doctrine; the man who does not possess it is to be expelled and must forfeit all his rights; if he be a fellow-countryman, he must be treated as a leper and lose all connexion with his nation. This fanaticism, which still flares up here and there in the Greek Church even to-day and in principle has not been abandoned, is not Greek, although a certain inclination towards it was not lacking in the ancient Greeks; still less did it originate in Roman law; it is the result, rather, of an unfortunate combination of several factors. When the Roman empire became Christian, the hard fight for existence which the Church had waged with the Gnostics was not yet forgotten; still less had the Church forgotten the last bloody persecutions which the State had inflicted upon it in a kind of despair. These two circumstances would in themselves be sufficient to explain how the Church came to feel that it had a right of reprisal, and was at the same time bound to suppress heretics. But, in addition, there had now appeared in the highest place, since the days of Diocletian and Constantine, the absolutist conception, derived from the East, of the unlimited right and the unlimited duty of the ruler in regard to his "subjects." The unfortunate factor in the great change was that the Roman Emperor was at once, and almost in the same moment, a Christian Emperor and an oriental despot. The more conscientious he was, the more intolerant he was bound to be ; for the deity had committed to his care not only men's bodies but their souls as well. Thus arose the aggressive and all-devouring orthodoxy of State and Church, or, rather, of the State-Church. Examples which were to hand from the Old Testament completed and sanctified the process.

Intolerance is a new growth in the land of the Greeks and cannot be roundly laid to their charge ; but the way in which doctrine developed, namely, as a philosophy of God and the world, was due to their influence ; and the fact that religion and doctrine were directly identified is also a product of the Greek spirit. No mere reference to the significance which doctrine already possessed in the apostolic age, and to the tendencies operating in the direction of bringing it into a speculative form, is sufficient to explain the change. These are matters, as I hope that I have shown in the previous lectures, which are rather to be understood in a different sense. It is in the second century, and with the apologists, that Intellectualism commences ; and, supported by the struggle with the Gnostics and by the Alexandrian school of religious philosophers in the Church, it manages to prevail.

But it is not enough to assess the teaching of

the Greek Church by its formal side alone, and ascertain in what way and to what extent it is exhibited, and what is the value to be placed upon it. We must also examine its substance; for it possesses two elements which are quite peculiar to it and separate it from the Greek philosophy of religion—*the idea of the creation*, and the doctrine of the *God-Man nature of the Saviour*. We shall treat of these two elements in our next lecture, and, further, of the two other elements which, side by side with tradition and doctrine, characterise the Greek Church; namely, the form of worship and the order of monkhood.

LECTURE XIII.

So far we have established the fact that Greek
Catholicism is characterised as a religion by two
elements : by *traditionalism* and by *intellectualism*.
According to traditionalism, the reverent preservation
of the received inheritance, and the defence of it
against all innovation, is not only an important duty,
but is itself the practical proof of religion. That is
an idea quite in harmony with antiquity and foreign
to the Gospel; for the Gospel knows absolutely
nothing of intercourse with God being bound up with
reverence for tradition itself. But the second element, intellectualism, is also of Greek origin. The
elaboration of the Gospel into a vast philosophy of
God and the world, in which every conceivable kind
of material is handled; the conviction that because
Christianity is the absolute religion it must give information on all questions of metaphysics, cosmology,
and history ; the view of revelation as a countless
multitude of doctrines and explanations, all equally
holy and important—this is Greek intellectualism.
According to it, *Knowledge* is the highest good, and
spirit is spirit only in so far as it knows ; everything

that is of an æsthetical, ethical, and religious character must be converted into some form of knowledge, which human will and life will then with certainty obey. The development of the Christian faith into an all-embracing theosophy, and the identification of faith with theological knowledge, are proofs that the Christian religion on Greek soil entered the proscribed circle of the native religious philosophy and has remained there.

But in this vast philosophy of God and the world, which possesses an absolute value as the "substance of what has been revealed" and as "orthodox doctrine," there are two elements which radically distinguish it from Greek religious philosophy and invest it with an entirely original character. I do not mean the appeal which it makes to revelation—for to that the Neoplatonists also appealed—but the *idea of creation* and the doctrine of *the God-Man nature of the Saviour*. They traverse the scheme of Greek religious philosophy at two critical points, and have therefore always been felt to be alien and intolerable by its genuine representatives.

The idea of creation we can deal with in a few words. It is undoubtedly an element which is as important as it is in thorough keeping with the Gospel. It abolishes all intertwining of God and world, and gives expression to the power and actuality of the living God. Attempts were not wanting, it is true, among Christian thinkers on Greek soil—just because they were Greeks—to conceive the Deity only as the uniform power operating in the fabric of the world, as the unity in diversity, and as its goal. Traces of this speculative idea are even still to be found in the Church doctrine; the idea of creation, however, triumphed, and therewith Christianity won a real victory.

The subject of the God-Man nature of the Saviour is one on which it is much more difficult to arrive at a correct opinion. It is indubitably the central point in the whole dogmatic system of the Greek Church. It supplied the doctrine of the Trinity. In the Greek view these two doctrines together make up Christian teaching *in nuce*. When a Father of the Greek Church once said, as he did say: "The idea of the God-Man nature, the idea of God becoming a man, is what is new in the new, nay, is the only new thing under the sun," not only did he correctly represent the opinion of all his fellow-believers, but he also at the same time strikingly expressed their view that, while sound intelligence and earnest reflection yield all the other points of doctrine of themselves, this one lies beyond them. The theologians of the Greek Church are convinced that the only real distinction between the Christian creed and natural philosophy is that the former embraces the doctrine of the God-Man nature, including the Trinity. Side by side with this, the only other doctrine that can at most come in question is that of the idea of creation.

If that be so, it is of radical importance to obtain a

correct view of the origin, meaning, and value of this doctrine. In its completed form it must look strange to anyone who comes to it straight from the evangelists. While no historical reflection can rid us of the impression that the whole fabric of ecclesiastical Christology is a thing absolutely outside the concrete personality of Jesus Christ, historical considerations nevertheless enable us not only to explain its origin but also even to justify, in a certain degree, the way in which it is formulated. Let us try to get a clear idea of the leading points.

We saw in a previous lecture how it came about that the Church teachers selected the conception of the Logos in order to define Christ's nature and majesty. They found the conception of the "Messiah" quite unintelligible; it conveyed no meaning to them. As conceptions cannot be improvised, they had to choose between representing Christ as a deified man, that is to say, as a hero, or conceiving his nature after the pattern of one of the Greek gods, or identifying it with the Logos. The first two possibilities had to be put aside, as they were "heathenish," or seemed to be so. There remained, therefore, the Logos. How well this formula served different purposes we have already pointed out. Did it not readily admit of being combined with the conception of the Sonship, without leading to any objectionable theogonies? It involved, too, no menace to monotheism. But the formula had a logic of its own, and this logic led to results which were not absolutely free from suspicion. The conception of the Logos was susceptible of very varied expression ; in spite of its sublime meaning, it could be also so conceived as to permit of the bearer of the title not being by any means of a truly divine nature but possessing one that was only half divine.

The question as to the more exact definition of the nature of the Logos-Christ could not have attained the enormous significance which it received in the Church, and might have been stilled by various speculative answers, if it had not been accompanied by the triumph of a very precise idea of the nature of redemption, which acted as a peremptory challenge. Among all the possible ideas on the subject of redemption—forgiveness of sins, release from the power of the demons, and so on—that idea came victoriously to the front in the Church in the third century which conceived of it as *redemption from death and therewith as elevation to the divine life, that is to say, as deification.* It is true that this conception found a safe starting-point in the Gospel, and support in the Pauline theology ; but in the form in which it was now developed it was foreign to both of them and conceived on Greek lines ; *mortality is in itself reckoned as the greatest evil, and as the cause of all evil, while the greatest of blessings is to live for ever.* What a severely Greek idea this is we can see, in the first place, from the fact that redemption from death is presented, in a wholly realistic fashion, as a *pharmacological* process

—the divine nature has to flow in and transform the mortal nature—and, in the second, from the way in which eternal life and deification were identified. But if actual interference in the constitution of human nature and its deification are involved, then *the redeemer must himself be God and must become man.* It is only on this condition that so marvellous a process can be imagined as actually taking place. Word, doctrine, individual deeds, are here of no avail —how can life be given to a stone, or a mortal made immortal, by preaching at them? Only when the divine itself bodily enters into mortality can mortality be transformed. It is not, however, the hero, but God Himself alone, who possesses the divine, that is to say, eternal life, and so possesses it as to permit of His *giving it to others.* The Logos, then, must be God Himself, and He must have actually become man. With the satisfying of these two conditions, real, natural redemption, that is to say, the deification of humanity, is actually effected. These considerations enable us to understand the prodigious disputes over the nature of the Logos-Christ which filled several centuries. They explain why Athanasius strove for the formula that the Logos-Christ was of the same nature as the Father, as though the existence or non-existence of the Christian religion were at stake. They show clearly how it was that other teachers in the Greek Church regarded any menace to the complete *unity* of the divine and the human in the Redeemer, any notion of a merely moral connexion, as a death-blow to Christianity. These teachers secured their formulas, which for them were anything but scholastic conceptions; rather, they were the statement and establishment of a matter of fact, in the absence of which the Christian religion was as unsatisfactory as any other. The doctrines of the identical nature of the three persons of the Trinity—how the doctrine of the Holy Ghost came about, I need not mention—and of the God-Man nature of the Redeemer are in strict accordance with the distinguishing notion of the redemption as a deification of man's nature by making him immortal. Without the help of the notion those formulas would never have been attained; but they also stand and fall with it. They prevailed, however, not because they were akin to the ideas of Greek philosophy, but because they were contrasted with them. Greek philosophy never ventured, and never aspired, to meet, in any similar way by "history" and speculative ideas, that wish for immortality which it so vividly entertained. To attribute any such interference with the Cosmos to an *historical* personality and the manner in which it appeared, and to ascribe to that personality a transformation in what, given once for all, was in a state of eternal flux, must necessarily have seemed, to Greek philosophy, pure mythology and superstition. The "only new thing under the sun" must necessarily have appeared to it, and did appear, to be the worst kind of fable.

The Greek Church still entertains the conviction to-day that in these doctrines it possesses the essence of Christianity, regarded at once as a mystery and as a mystery that has been revealed. Criticism of this contention is not difficult. We must acknowledge that those doctrines powerfully contributed to keeping the Christian religion from dissolving into Greek religious philosophy; further, that they profoundly impress us with the absolute character of this religion; again, that they are in actual accordance with the Greek notion of redemption; lastly, that this very notion has *one* of its roots in the Gospel. But beyond this we can acknowledge nothing; nay, it is to be observed (i.) that the notion of the redemption as a deification of mortal nature is subchristian, because the moral element involved can at best be only tacked on to it; (ii.) that the whole doctrine is inadmissible, because it has scarcely any connexion with the Jesus Christ of the Gospel, and its formulas do not fit him; it is, therefore, not founded in truth; and (iii.) that as it is connected with the real Christ only by uncertain threads, it leads us away from him; it does not keep his image alive, but, on the contrary, demands that this image should be apprehended solely in the light of alleged hypotheses about him expressed in theoretical propositions. That this substitution produces no very serious or destructive effects is principally owing to the fact that in spite of them the Church has not suppressed the Gospels, and that their own innate power makes itself felt. It may also be conceded that the notion of God having become man does not everywhere produce the effect only of a bewildering mystery, but, on the contrary, is capable of leading to the pure and definite conviction that God was in Christ. We may admit, lastly, that the egoistic desire for immortal existence will, within the Christian sphere, experience a moral purification through the longing *to live with and in God*, and to remain inseparably bound to His love. But all these admissions cannot do away with the palpable fact that in Greek dogma we have a fatal connexion established between the desire of the ancients for immortal life and the Christian message. Nor can anyone deny that this connexion, implanted in Greek religious philosophy and the intellectualism which characterised it, has led to formulas which are incorrect, introduce a supposititious Christ in the place of the real one, and, besides, encourage the delusion that, if only a man possesses the right formula, he has the thing itself. Even though the Christological formula were the theologically right one—what a departure from the Gospel is involved in maintaining that a man can have no relation with Jesus Christ, nay, that he is sinning against him and will be cast out, unless he first of all acknowledges that Christ was *one* person with two natures and two powers of will, one of them divine and one human. Such is the demand into which intellectualism has developed. Can such a system

still find a place for the Gospel story of the Syro-
phœnician woman or the centurion at Capernaum ?

But with traditionalism and intellectualism a
further element is associated, namely, ritualism.
If religion is presented as a complex system of
traditional doctrine, to which the few alone have
any real access, the majority of believers cannot
practise it at all except as ritual. Doctrine
comes to be administered in stereotyped formulas
accompanied by symbolic acts. Although no inner
understanding of it is thus possible, it produces
the feeling of something mysterious. The very
deification which the future is expected to bring,
and which in itself is something that can neither
be described nor conceived, is now administered as
though it were an earnest of what is to come, by
means of ritual acts. An imaginative mood is excited,
and disposes to its reception; and this excitement,
when enhanced, is its seal.

Such are the feelings which move the members
of the Greek Catholic Church. Intercourse with
God is achieved through the cult of a mystery, and
by means of hundreds of efficacious formulas small
and great, signs, pictures, and consecrated acts,
which, if punctiliously and submissively observed,
communicate divine grace and prepare the Christian
for eternal life. Doctrine as such is for the most
part something unknown; if it appears at all, it
is only in the form of liturgical aphorisms. For

ninety-nine per cent. of these Christians, religion
exists only as a ceremonious ritual, in which it is
externalised. But even for Christians of advanced
intelligence all these ritual acts are absolutely necessary, for it is only in them that doctrine receives
its correct application and obtains its due result.

There is no sadder spectacle than this transformation of the Christian religion from a worship
of God in spirit and in truth into a worship of
God in signs, formulas, and idols. To feel the whole
pity of this development, we need not descend to
such adherents of this form of Christendom as are
religiously and intellectually in a state of complete
abandonment, like the Copts and Abyssinians; the
Syrians, Greeks, and Russians are, taken as a whole,
only a little better. Where, however, can we find
in Jesus' message even a trace of any injunction
that a man is to submit to solemn ceremonies as
though they were mysterious ministrations, to be
punctilious in observing a ritual, to put up pictures,
and to mumble maxims and formulas in a prescribed
fashion? *It was to destroy this sort of religion
that Jesus Christ suffered himself to be nailed to
the cross*, and now we find it re-established under
his name and authority! Not only has "mysta-
gogy" stepped into a position side by side with
the "mathesis," that is to say, the doctrine, which
called it forth; but the truth is that "doctrine"—
be its constitution what it may, it is still a spiritual
principle—has disappeared, and ceremony dominates

everything. This is what marks the relapse into the ancient form of the lowest class of religion. Over the vast area of Greek and Oriental Christendom religion has been almost stifled by ritualism. It is not that religion has sacrificed one of its essential elements. No! it has entered an entirely different plane; it has descended to the level where religion may be described as a cult and nothing but a cult.

Nevertheless, Greek and Oriental Christianity contains within itself an element which for centuries has been capable of offering, and still offers here and there to-day, a certain resistance to the combined forces of traditionalism, intellectualism, and ritualism—I mean monasticism. To the question, Who is in the highest sense of the word a Christian? the Greek Christian replies : the monk. The man who practises silence and purity, who shuns not only the world but also the Church of the world, who avoids not only false doctrine but any statement about the true, who fasts, gives himself up to contemplation, and steadily waits for God's glorious light to dawn upon his gaze, who attaches no value to anything but tranquillity and meditation on the Eternal, who asks nothing of life but death, and who from such utter unselfishness and purity makes mercy arise—this is the Christian. To him not even the Church and the consecration which it bestows is an absolute necessity. For such a man the whole system of sanctified secularity has vanished. Over

and over again in ascetics of this kind the Church
has seen in its ranks figures of such strength and
delicacy of religious feeling, so filled with the divine,
so inwardly active in forming themselves after certain
features of Christ's image, that we may, indeed,
say : here there is a living religion, not unworthy
of Christ's name. We Protestants must not take
direct offence at the form of monasticism. The
conditions under which our Churches arose have
made a harsh and one-sided opinion of it a kind
of duty. And although for the present, and in
view of the problems which press on us, we may
be justified in retaining this opinion, we must not
summarily apply it to other circumstances. Nothing
but monasticism could provide a leaven and a coun-
terpoise in that traditionalistic and ritualistic secular
Church, such as the Greek Church was and still is.
Here there was freedom, independence, and vivid
experience ; here the truth that it is only what is
experienced and comes from within that has any
value in religion carried the day.

And yet, the invaluable tension which in this part of
Christendom existed between the secular Church and
monasticism has unhappily almost disappeared, and
of the blessing which it established there is scarcely
a trace left. Not only has monasticism become
subject to the Church and is everywhere bent
under its yoke, but the secular spirit has in a
special degree invaded the monasteries. Greek
and oriental monks are now, as a rule, the

instruments of the lowest and worst functions of the Church, of the worship of pictures and relics, of the crassest superstition and the most imbecile sorcery. Exceptions are not wanting, and it is still to the monks that we must pin our hopes of a better future; but it is not easy to see how a Church is to be reformed which, teach what it will, is content with its adherents finding the Christian *faith* in the observance of certain ceremonies, and Christian *morality* in keeping fast-days correctly.

As to our last question: What modifications did the Gospel undergo in this Church and how did it hold its own? Well, in the first place, I do not expect to be contradicted if I answer that this official ecclesiasticism with its priests and its cult, with all its vessels, saints, vestments, pictures and amulets, with its ordinances of fasting and its festivals, has absolutely nothing to do with the religion of Christ. It is the religion of the ancient world, tacked on to certain conceptions in the Gospel; or, rather, it is the ancient religion with the Gospel absorbed into it. The religious moods which are here produced, or which turn towards this kind of religion are, in so far as they can still be called religious at all, of a class lower than Christian. But neither have its traditionalism and its "orthodoxy" much in common with the Gospel; they, too, were not derived from it and cannot be traced back to it. Correct doctrine, reverence,

obedience, the shudderings of awe, may be valuable
and edifying things ; they may avail to bind and
restrain the individual, especially when they draw
him into the community of a stable society ; but
they have nothing to do with the Gospel, as long
as they fail to touch the individual at the point
where freedom lies, and inner decision for or against
God.   In contrast with this, monasticism, in its
resolve to serve God by an ascetic and contemplative
life, contains an incomparably more valuable element,
because sayings of Christ, even though applied in
a one-sided and limited way, are nevertheless taken
as a standard, and the possibility of an independent
inner life being kindled is not so far removed.

Not so far removed—entirely lacking, thank God,
it is not, even in the waste shrines of this
ecclesiasticism, and Christ's sayings sound in the
ear of any who visit its churches.   On the Church
as a Church, apparatus and all, there is nothing
more favourable to be said than has been said
already ; the best thing about it is that it keeps
up, although to a modest extent, the knowledge
of the Gospel.   Jesus' words, even though only
mumbled by the priests, take the first place in
this Church, too, and the quiet mission which
they pursue is not suppressed.   Side by side with
the magical apparatus and the transports of feeling,
of which the ceremony is only the *caput mortuum*,
stand Jesus' sayings ; they are read in private and
in public, and no superstition avails to destroy

their power. Nor can its fruits be mistaken by
anyone who will look below the surface. Among
these Christians, too, priests and laity, there are
men who have come to know God as the Father
of mercy and the leader of their lives, and who
love Jesus Christ, not because they know him as
the person with two natures, but because a ray
of his being has shone from the Gospel into their
hearts, and this ray has become light and warmth
to their own lives. And although the idea of the
fatherly providence of God more readily assumes
an almost fatalistic form in the East, and produces
too much quietism, it is certain that here, too, it
endows men with strength and energy, unselfishness
and love. I need only refer again to Tolstoi's
Village Tales, which I have already quoted. The
picture which they present is not artificial. But
from much also that I have myself seen and experienced I can testify how even with the Russian
peasant or the humbler priests, in spite of all the
Saint- and picture-worship, a power of simple trust
in God is to be found, a delicacy of moral feeling,
and an active brotherly love, which does not dis-
claim its origin in the Gospel. Where they exist,
however, the entire ceremonial service of religion
is capable of undergoing a spiritualisation, not by
any "symbolical re-interpretation"—that is much
too artificial a process—but because, if only the soul
is touched by the living God at all, thought can
rise to him even by the help of an idol.

But it is truly no accidental circumstance that, in so far as any independent religious life is to be found among the members of this Church, it at once takes shape in trust in God, in humility, in unselfishness and mercy, and that Jesus Christ is at the same time laid hold of with reverence; for these are just the indications which show us that the Gospel is not as yet stifled, and that it is in these religious virtues that it has its real substance.

As a whole and in its structure the system of the oriental Churches is foreign to the Gospel; it means at once a veritable transformation of the Christian faith and the depression of religion to a much lower level, namely, that of the ancient world. But in its monasticism, in so far as this is not entirely subject to the secular Church and itself secularised, there is an element which reduces the whole ecclesiastical apparatus to a secondary position, and which opens up the possibility of attaining a state of Christian independence. Above all, however, by not having suppressed the Gospel, but by having kept it accessible, even though in a meagre fashion, the Church still possesses the corrective in its midst. Side by side with the Church the Gospel exercises its own influence on individuals. This influence, however, takes shape in a type of religion exhibiting the very characteristics which we have shown to be most distinctive of Jesus' message. Thus on the ground occupied by this

Church the Gospel has not completely perished. Here, too, human souls find a dependence on God and a freedom in Him, and when they have found these, they speak the language which every Christian understands, and which goes to every Christian's heart.

LECTURE XIV.

The Christian Religion in Roman Catholicism.

The Roman Church is the most comprehensive and the vastest, the most complicated and yet at the same time the most uniform structure which, as far as we know, history has produced. All the powers of the human mind and soul, and all the elemental forces at mankind's disposal, have had a hand in creating it. In its many-sided character and severe cohesion Roman Catholicism is far in advance of Greek. We ask, in turn :—

What did the Roman Catholic Church achieve?

What are its characteristics?

What modifications has the Gospel suffered in this Church, and how much of it has remained?

What did the Roman Catholic Church achieve? Well, in the first place, it educated the Romano-Germanic nations, and educated them in a sense other than that in which the Eastern Church educated the Greeks, Slavs, and Orientals. However much their original nature, or primitive and historical circumstances, may have favoured those nations and helped to promote their rise, the value of the services which the Church rendered is not thereby diminished. It brought Christian civilisation to young nations, and brought it, not once only, so as to keep them at its first stage—no ! it gave them something which was capable of exercising a progressive educational influence, and for a period of almost a thousand years it itself led the advance. Up to the fourteenth century it was a leader and a mother; it supplied the ideas, set the aims, and disengaged the forces. Up to the fourteenth century— thenceforward, as we may see, those whom it educated became independent, and struck out paths which it did not indicate, and on which it is neither willing nor able to follow them. But even so, however, during the period covered by the last six hundred years, it has not fallen so far behind as the Greek Church. With comparatively brief interruptions it has proved itself fully a match for the whole movement of politics—we in Germany know that well enough !—and even in the movement of thought it still has an important share. The time, of course, is long past since it was a leader; on the contrary, it is now a drag; but, in view of the mistaken and precipitate elements in modern progress, the drag which it supplies is not always the reverse of a blessing.

In the second place, however, this Church upheld the idea of religious and ecclesiastical independence in Western Europe in the face of the tendencies,

not lacking here either, towards State-omnipotence
in the spiritual domain. In the Greek Church, as
we saw, religion has become so intimately allied with
nationality and the State that, public worship and
monasticism apart, it has no room left for independent action. On Western ground it is otherwise ;
the religious element and the moral element bound
up with it occupy an independent sphere and
jealously guard it. This we owe in the main to
the Roman Church.

These two facts embrace the most important piece
of work which this Church achieved and in part still
achieves. We have already indicated the bounds
which must be set to the first. To the second also
a sensible limitation attaches, and we shall see what
it is as we proceed.

What are the characteristics of the Roman
Church ? This was our second question. Unless I
am mistaken, the Church, complicated as it is, may
be resolved into three chief elements. The first,
Catholicism, it shares with the Greek Church. The
second is the *Latin spirit* and the *Roman World-
Empire* continuing in the Roman Church. The third
is the spirit and religious fervour of *St. Augustine.*
So far as the inner life of this Church is religious life
and religious thought, it follows the standard which
St. Augustine authoritatively fixed. Not only has
he arisen again and again in his many successors,
but he has awakened and kindled numbers of men

who, coming forward with independent religious and theological fervour, are nevertheless spirit of his spirit.

These three elements, the Catholic, the Latin in the sense of the Roman World-Empire, and the Augustinian, constitute the peculiar character of the Roman Church.

So far as the first is concerned, you may recognise its importance by the fact that the Roman Church to-day receives every Greek Christian, nay, at once effects a "union" with every Greek ecclesiastical community, without more ado, as soon as the Pope is acknowledged and submission is made to his apostolic supremacy. Any other condition that may be exacted from the Greek Christians is of absolutely no moment; they are even allowed to retain divine worship in their mother tongue, and married priests. If we consider what a "purification" Protestants have to undergo before they can be received into the bosom of the Roman Church, the difference is obvious. Now a Church cannot make so great a mistake about itself as to omit any essential condition in taking up new members, especially if they come from another confession. The element which the Roman Church shares with the Greek must, then, be of significant and critical importance, when it is sufficient to make union possible on the condition that the papal supremacy is recognised. As a matter of fact, the main points characteristic of Greek Catholicism are all to be found in Roman as well, and are, on occasion, just as energetically maintained here as they are there. Traditionalism, orthodoxy, and ritualism play just the same part here as they do there, so far as "higher considerations" do not step in; and the same is true of monasticism also.

So far as "higher considerations" do not step in—here we have already passed to the examination of the second element, namely, the Latin Spirit in the sense of the Roman World-dominion. In the Western half of Christendom the Latin spirit, the spirit of Rome, very soon effected certain distinct modifications in the general Catholic idea. As early as the beginning of the third century we see the thought emerging in the Latin Fathers that salvation, however effected and whatever its nature, is bestowed in the form of a contract under definite conditions, and only to the extent to which they are observed; it is *salus legitima*; in fixing these conditions the Deity manifested its mercy and indulgence, but it guards their observance all the more jealously. Further, the whole contents of revelation are *lex*, the Bible as well as tradition. Again, this tradition is attached to a class of officials and to their correct succession. The "mysteries," however, are "sacraments"; that is to say, on the one hand, they are binding acts; on the other, they contain definite gifts of grace in a carefully limited form and with a specific application. Again, the discipline of penance is a procedure laid down by law and akin to the process adopted in a civil action or a suit in defence of honour. Lastly, the Church is a *legal institution*; and it is so, not side by side with its function of preserving and distributing salvation, but it is a legal institution for the sake of this very function.

But it is in its constitution as a Church that it is a legal establishment. We must briefly see how things stand in regard to this constitution, as its foundations are common to the Eastern and the Western Church. When the monarchical episcopate had developed, the Church began to approximate its constitution to State government. The system of uniting sees under a metropolitan who was, as a rule, the bishop of the provincial capital, corresponded with the distribution of the Empire into provinces. Above and beyond this, the ecclesiastical constitution in the East was developed a step further when it adapted itself to the division of the Empire introduced by Diocletian, by which large groups of provinces were united. Thus arose the constitution of the patriarchate, which was not, however, strictly enforced, and was in part counteracted by other considerations.

In the West no division into patriarchates came about; but on the other hand something else happened: in the fifth century the Western Roman Empire perished of internal weakness and through the inroads of the barbarians. What was left of what was Roman took refuge in the Roman Church —civilisation, law, and orthodox faith as opposed to the Arian. The barbarian chiefs, however, did not venture to set themselves up as Roman Emperors, and enter the vacant shrine of the *imperium*; they founded empires of their own in the provinces. In these circumstances the Bishop of Rome appeared as the guardian of the past and the shield of the future. All over the provinces occupied by the barbarians, even in those which had previously maintained a defiant independence in the face of Rome, bishops and laity looked to him. Whatever Roman elements the barbarians and Arians left standing in the provinces —and they were not few—were ecclesiasticised and at the same time put under the protection of the Bishop of Rome, who was the chief person there after the Emperor's disappearance. But in Rome the episcopal throne was occupied in the fifth century by men who understood the signs of the times and utilised them to the full. *The Roman Church in this way privily pushed itself into the place of the Roman World-Empire, of which it is the actual continuation:* the empire has not perished, but has only undergone a transformation. If we assert, and mean the assertion to hold good even of the present time, that the Roman Church is the old Roman Empire consecrated by the Gospel, that is no mere "clever remark," but the recognition of the true state of the matter historically, and the most appropriate and fruitful way of describing the character of this Church. It still governs the nations; its Popes rule like Trajan and Marcus Aurelius; Peter and

Paul have taken the place of Romulus and Remus; the bishops and archbishops, of the proconsuls; the troops of priests and monks correspond to the legions; the Jesuits, to the imperial body-guard. The continued influence of the old Empire and its institutions may be traced in detail, down to individual legal ordinances, nay, even in the very clothes. That is no Church like the evangelical communities, or the national Churches of the East; it is a political creation, and as imposing as a World-Empire, because the continuation of the Roman Empire. The Pope, who calls himself "King" and "Pontifex Maximus," is Cæsar's successor. The Church, which as early as the third and fourth century was entirely filled with the Roman spirit, has re-established in itself the Roman Empire. Nor have patriotic Catholics in Rome and Italy in every century from the seventh and eighth onwards understood the matter otherwise. When Gregory VII. entered upon the struggle with the imperial power, this is the way in which an Italian prelate fired his ardour:

> *Seize the first Apostle's sword,*
> *Peter's glowing sword, and smite !*
> *Scatter far the savage horde ;*
> *Break their wild, impetuous might !*
> *Let them feel the yoke of yore,*
> *Let them bear it evermore !*
>
> *What with blood in Marius' day,*
> *Marius and his soldiers brave,*

Or by Julius' mighty sway,
  Romans did their land to save ;
Thou canst do by simple word.
  Great the Church's holy sword !

Rome made great again by thee
  Offers all thy meed of praise ;
Not for Scipio's victory
  Did it louder pæans raise,
Nor entwine the laurel crown
  For a deed of more renown.

Who is it that is thus addressed, a bishop or a
Cæsar ?   A Cæsar, I imagine; it was felt to be so
then, and it is still felt to be so to-day.   It is an
Empire that this priestly Cæsar rules, and to attack
it with the armament of dogmatic polemics alone is
to beat the air.

I cannot here show what immense results follow
from the fact that the Catholic Church is the Roman
Empire.   Let me mention only a few conclusions
which the Church itself draws.   It is just as essential
to this Church to exercise governmental power as
to proclaim the Gospel.   The phrase " Christus
vincit, Christus regnat, Christus triumphat," must
be understood in a political sense.   He rules on
earth by the fact that his Rome-directed Church
rules, and rules, too, by law and by force ; that is to
say, it employs all the means of which States avail
themselves.   Accordingly it recognises no form of religious fervour which does not first of all submit to
this papal Church, is approved by it, and remains in

constant dependence upon it. This Church, then, teaches its "subjects" to say : "Though I understand all mysteries, and though I have all faith, and though I bestow all my goods to feed the poor, and though I give my body to be burned, and have not unity in love which alone floweth from unconditional obedience to the Church, it profiteth me nothing." Outside the pale of the Church, all faith, all love, all the virtues, even martyrdoms, are of no value whatever. Naturally ; for even an earthly State appreciates only those services which a man has rendered for its sake. But here the State identifies itself with the kingdom of Heaven, in other respects proceeding just like other States. From this fact you can yourselves deduce all the Church's claims ; they follow without difficulty. Even the most exorbitant demand appears quite natural as soon as you only admit the truth of the two leading propositions : "The Roman Church is the kingdom of God," and "The Church must govern like an earthly State." It is not to be denied that Christian motives have also had a hand in this development—the desire to bring the Christian religion into a real connexion with life, and to make its influence felt in every situation that may arise, as well as anxiety for the salvation of individuals and of nations. How many earnest Catholic Christians there have been who had no other real desire than to establish Christ's rule on earth and build up his kingdom ! But while there can be no doubt that their intention, and the energy with which they put their hands to the work, made them superior to the Greeks, there can be as little that it is a serious misunderstanding of Christ's and the apostles' injunctions to aim at establishing and building up the kingdom of God by political means. The only forces which this kingdom knows are religious and moral forces, and it rests on a basis of freedom. But when a Church comes forward with the claims of an earthly State, it is bound to make use of all the means at the disposal of that State, including, therefore, crafty diplomacy and force; for the earthly State, even a State governed by law, must on occasion become a State that acts contrary to law. The course of development which this Church has followed as an earthly State was, then, bound to lead logically to the absolute monarchy of the Pope and his infallibility; for in an earthly theocracy infallibility means, at bottom, nothing more than full sovereignty means in a secular State. That the Church has not shrunk from drawing this last conclusion is a proof of the extent to which the sacred element in it has become secularised.

That this second element was bound to produce a radical change in the characteristic features of Catholicism in Western Europe, in its traditionalism, its orthodoxy, its ritualism, and its monasticism, is obvious. Traditionalism holds the same position after the change as it did before; but when any element in it has become inconvenient, it is dropped and its place taken by the papal will. " La tradition, c'est moi," as Pius IX. is reported to have said. Further, " sound doctrine " is still a leading principle, but, as a matter of fact, it can be altered by the ecclesiastical policy of the Pope ; subtle distinctions have given many a dogma a new meaning. New dogmas, too, are promulgated. In many respects doctrine has become more arbitrary, and a rigid formula in a matter of dogma may be set aside by a contrary injunction in a matter of ethics and in the confessional. The hard and fast lines of the past can be everywhere relaxed in favour of the needs of the present. The same holds good of ritualism, as also of monasticism. The extent to which the old monasticism has been altered, by no means always to its disadvantage alone, and has even in some important aspects been transformed into its flat opposite, I cannot here show. In its organisation this Church possesses a faculty of adapting itself to the course of history such as no other Church possesses ; it always remains the same old Church, or seems to do so, and is always becoming a new one.

The third element determining the character of the spirit prevalent in the Church is opposed to that which we have just discussed, and yet has held its own side by side with the second : it goes by the names of Augustine and Augustinianism. In the fifth century, at the very time when the Church

was setting itself to acquire the inheritance of the
Roman Empire, it came into possession of a religious
genius of extraordinary depth and power, accepted his
ideas and feelings, and up to the present day has been
unable to get rid of them.   That the Church became
at one and the same time Cæsarian and Augustinian is
the most important and marvellous fact in its history.
What kind of a spirit, however, and what kind of a
tendency, did it receive from Augustine?

Well, in the first place, Augustine's theology and
his religious fervour denote a special resuscitation
of the Pauline experience and doctrine of sin and
grace, of guilt and justification, of divine predestination and human servitude.   In the centuries that
had elapsed since the apostle's day this experience
and the doctrine embodying it had been lost, but
Augustine went through the same inner experiences
as Paul, gave them the same sort of expression, and
clothed them in definite conceptions.   There was no
question here of mere imitation ; the individual differences between the two cases are of the utmost importance, especially in the way in which the doctrine of
justification is conceived.   With Augustine, it was
represented as a constant process, continuing until
love and all the virtues completely filled the heart ;
but, as with Paul, it is all a matter of individual
experience and inner life.   If you read Augustine's
Confessions you will acknowledge that in spite of
all the rhetoric—and rhetoric there is—it is the work
of a genius who has felt God, the God of the Spirit,

to be the be-all and the end-all of his life; who thirsts after Him and desires nothing beside Him. Further, all the sad and terrible experiences which he had had in his own person, all the rupture with himself, all the service of transient things, the "crumbling away into the world bit by bit," and the egoism for which he had to pay in loss of strength and freedom, he reduces to the one root, *sin*; that is to say, lack of communion with God, godlessness. Again, what released him from the entanglements of the world, from selfishness and inner decay, and gave him strength, freedom, and a consciousness of the Eternal, he calls, with Paul, *grace*. With him he feels, too, that grace is wholly the work of God, but that it is obtained through and by Christ, and possessed as forgiveness of sins and as the spirit of love. He is much less free and more beset with scruples in his view of sin than the great apostle; and it is this which gives his religious language and everything that proceeded from him quite a peculiar colour. "Forgetting those things which are behind, and reaching forth unto those things which are before"— the apostolic maxim is not Augustine's. *Consolation for the misery of sin*—this is the complexion of his entire Christianity. Only rarely was he capable of soaring to the sense of the glorious liberty of the children of God; and, where he was so capable, he could not testify to it in the same way as Paul. But he could express the sense of consolation for the misery of sin with a strength of feeling and in words of an overwhelming force such as no one before him ever displayed; nay, more: he has managed by what he has written to go so straight to the souls of millions, to describe so precisely their inner condition, and so impressively and overpoweringly to put the consolation before them, that what he felt has been felt again and again for fifteen hundred years. Up to the day in which we live, so far as Catholic Christians are concerned, inward and vivid religious fervour, and the expression which it takes, are in their whole character Augustinian. It is by what he felt that they are kindled, and it is his thoughts that they think. Nor is it otherwise with many Protestants, and those not of the worst kind. This juxtaposition of sin and grace, this interconnexion of feeling and doctrine, seems to possess an indestructible power which no lapse of time is able to touch; this feeling of mixed pain and bliss is an unforgettable possession with those who have once experienced it; and even though they may have subsequently emancipated themselves from religion it remains for them a sacred memory.

The Western Church opened, and was compelled to open, its doors to this Augustine at the very moment when it was preparing to enter upon its dominion. It was defenceless in face of him; it had so little of any real value to offer from its immediate past that it weakly capitulated. Thus arose the astonishing "complexio oppositorum" which we see in Western Catholicism: the Church of rites, of law, of politics, of world-dominion, and the Church in which a highly individual, delicate, sublimated sense and doctrine of sin and grace is brought into play. The external and the internal elements are supposed to unite! To speak frankly, this has been impossible from the beginning; internal tension and conflict were bound to arise at once; the history of Western Catholicism is full of it. Up to a certain point, however, these antitheses admit of being reconciled; they admit of it at least so far as the same men are concerned. That is proved by no less a person than Augustine himself, who, in addition to his other characteristics, was also a staunch Churchman; nay, who in such matters as power and prestige promoted the external interests of the Church, and its equipment as a whole, with the greatest energy. I cannot here explain how he managed to accomplish this work, but that there could be no lack of internal contradictions in it is obvious. Only let us be clear about two facts : firstly, that the outward Church is more and more forcing the inward Augustinianism into the background, and transforming and modifying it, without, however, being able wholly to destroy it; secondly, that all the great personalities who have continued to kindle religious fervour afresh in the Western Church, and to purify and deepen it, have directly or indirectly proceeded from Augustine and formed themselves on him. The long chain of Catholic reformers, from Agobard and Claudius of Turin in the ninth century down to the Jansenists in the seventeenth and eighteenth, and beyond them, is Augustinian.   And if the Council of Trent may be in many respects rightly called a Council of Reform ; if the doctrine of penance and grace was formulated then with much more depth and inwardness than could be expected from the state of Catholic theology in the fourteenth and fifteenth centuries, that is only owing to the continued influence of Augustine.   With the doctrine of grace taken from Augustine, the Church has, indeed, associated a practice of the confessional which threatens to make that doctrine absolutely ineffective.   But, however far it may stretch its bounds so as to keep all those within its pale who do not revolt against its authority, it after all not only tolerates such as take the same view of sin and grace as Augustine, but it also desires that, wherever possible, everyone may feel as strongly as he the gravity of sin and the blessedness of belonging to God.

Such are the essential elements of Roman Catholicism.   There is much else that might be mentioned, but what has been said denotes the leading points.

We pass to the last question : What modifications has the Gospel here undergone, and how much of it is left ?   Well—this is not a matter that needs many words—the whole outward and visible institution of a Church claiming divine dignity has no foundation whatever in the Gospel.   It is a case, not of distortion, but of total perversion.   Religion has here strayed away in a direction that is not its own.

As Eastern Catholicism may in many respects be more appropriately regarded as part of the history of Greek religion than of the history of the Gospel, so Roman Catholicism must be regarded as part of the history of the Roman World-Empire. To contend, as it does, that Christ founded a kingdom; that this kingdom is the Roman Church; that he equipped it with a sword, nay, with two swords, a spiritual and a temporal, is to secularise the Gospel; nor can this contention be sustained by appealing to the idea that Christ's spirit ought certainly to bear rule amongst mankind. The Gospel says, "Christ's kingdom is not of this world," but the Church has set up an earthly kingdom; Christ demands that his ministers shall not rule but serve, but here the priests govern the world; Christ leads his disciples away from political and ceremonious religion and places every man face to face with God —God and the soul, the soul and its God, but here, on the contrary, man is bound to an earthly institution with chains that cannot be broken, and he must obey; it is only when he obeys that he approaches God. There was a time when Roman Christians shed their blood because they refused to do worship to Cæsar, and rejected religion of the political kind; to-day they do not, indeed, actually pray to an earthly ruler, but they have subjected their souls to the despotic orders of the Roman papal King.

LECTURE XV.

THE point to which we referred at the close of the last lecture was that, as an outward and visible Church and a State founded on law and on force, Roman Catholicism has nothing to do with the Gospel, nay, is in fundamental contradiction with it. That this State has borrowed a divine lustre from the Gospel, and finds this lustre extraordinarily advantageous, cannot avail to upset the verdict. To mix the divine with the secular, and what is innermost in a man with a political element, is to work the greatest of mischiefs, because the conscience is thereby enslaved and religion robbed of its solemn character. It is inevitable that this character should be lost when every possible measure which serves to maintain the *earthly* empire of the Church—for example, the sovereignty of the Pope—is proclaimed as the divine will. We are reminded, however, that it is just this independent action on the part of the Church which saves religion in Western Europe from entirely degenerating into nationality, or the State, or police. The Church, it is urged, has maintained intact the high idea of the complete self-subsistence of religion and its independence of the State. We may admit the claim, but the price which Western Europe has had to pay for this service, and still pays, is much too great; by having to pay so heavy a tribute, the nations are threatened with bankruptcy *within*; and, as for the Church, the capital which it has amassed is truly a capital that consumes. With all the apparent increase in its power, a pauperising process is slowly being accomplished in the Church; slowly but surely. Let me here digress from our subject for a moment.

No one who looks at the present political situation can have any ground for asserting that the power of the Roman Church is on the wane. What a growth it has experienced in the nineteenth century! And yet—any one with a keen eye sees that the Church is far from possessing now such a plenitude of power as it enjoyed in the twelfth and thirteenth centuries, when all the material and spiritual forces available were at its disposal. Since that epoch its power has, in point of intensity, suffered an enormous decline, arrested by a few brief outbursts of enthusiasm between 1540 and 1620, and in the nineteenth century. Earnest Catholics, concerned at this fact, make no secret of it; they know and admit that an important portion of the spiritual possessions necessary to the dominion of the Church has been lost to it. And again; what is the position of the Latin nations which, when all is said, form the proper province of the Roman Church's rule? There is only one of them which can really be called a great Power, and what sort of spectacle will it present in another generation? As a State this Church lives to-day, to a not inconsiderable extent, on its history, its old Roman and mediæval history; and it lives as the Roman Empire of the Romans. But empires do not live for ever. Will the Church be capable of maintaining itself in the great changes to come? Will it bear the increasing tension between it and the intellectual life of the people? Will it survive the decline of the Latin nations?

But let us leave this question to answer itself. Let us recollect, rather, that this Church, thanks above all to its Augustinianism, possesses in its orders of monkhood and its religious societies a deep element of life in its midst. In all ages it has produced saints, so far as men can be so called, and it still produces them to-day. Trust in God, unaffected humility, the assurance of redemption, the devotion of one's life to the service of one's brethren, are to be found in it; many brethren take up the cross of Christ and exercise at one and the same time that self-judgment and that joy in God which Paul and Augustine achieved. The *Imitatio Christi* kindles independent religious life, and a fire which burns with a flame of its own. Ecclesiasticism has not availed to suppress the power of the Gospel, which, in spite of the frightful weight that it has to carry, makes its way again and again. It still works like leaven, nor can we fail to see that this Church, side by side with a lax morality for which it has often enough been to blame, has, by the mouth of its great mediæval theologians, fruitfully applied the Gospel to many circumstances of life and created a Christian ethics. Here and elsewhere it has proved that it not only carries, as it were, the thoughts of the Gospel with it, as a river carries grains of gold, but that they are bound up with it and have been further developed in it. The infallible Pope, the "Apostolico-Roman polytheism," the veneration of the Saints, blind obedience, and apathetic devotion — these things seem to have stifled all inwardness, and yet there are Christians still to be found in this Church, too, of the kind which the Gospel has awakened, earnest and loving, filled with joy and peace in God. Lastly, the mischief is not that the Gospel has been bound up with political forms at all—Melanchthon was no traitor when he expressed his willingness to acknowledge the Pope if he would permit the Gospel to be preached in its purity—but it lies in the *sanctification* of the political element, and in the inability of this Church to get rid of what was once of service in particular historical circumstances, but has now become an obstruction and a clog.

We now pass to the last section in the exposition of our subject.

The Christian Religion in Protestantism.

Anyone who looks at the external condition of Protestantism, especially in Germany, may, at first sight, well exclaim : "What a miserable spectacle!" But no one can survey the history of Europe from the second century to the present time without being forced to the conclusion that in the whole course of this history the greatest movement and the one most pregnant with good was the Reformation in the sixteenth century ; even the great change which took place at the transition to the nineteenth is inferior to it in importance. What do all our discoveries and inventions and our advances in outward civilisation signify in comparison with the fact that to-day there are thirty millions of Germans, and many more millions of Christians outside Germany, who possess a religion without priests, without sacrifices, without 'fragments' of grace, without ceremonies—a spiritual religion!

Protestantism must be understood, first and foremost, by the contrast which it offers to Catholicism, and here there is a double direction which any estimate of it must take, first as *Reformation* and secondly as *Revolution*. It was a reformation in regard to the doctrine of salvation ; a revolution in regard to the Church, its authority, and its apparatus. Hence Protestantism is no spontaneous phenomenon, created as it were by a "generatio equivoca"; but, as its very name implies, it was called into being by the misdeeds of the Roman Church having become intolerable. It was the close of a long series of cognate but ineffectual attempts at reform in the Middle Ages. If the position which it thus holds in history proves its continuity with the past, the fact is still more strongly in evidence in its own and not inappropriate contention that it was not an innovation in regard to religion, but a restoration and renewal of it. But from the point of view of the Church and its authority Protestantism was undoubtedly a revolutionary phenomenon. We must, then, take account of it in both these relations.

Protestantism was a *Reformation*, that is to say, a renewal, as regards the core of the matter, as regards religion, and consequently as regards the doctrine of salvation. That may be shown in the main in three points.

In the first place, religion was here brought back again to itself, in so far as the Gospel and the corresponding religious experience were put into the foreground and freed of all alien accretions. Religion was taken out of the vast and monstrous fabric which had been previously called by its name—a fabric embracing the Gospel and holy water, the priesthood of all believers and the Pope on his throne, Christ the Redeemer and St. Anne—and was *reduced* to its essential factors, to the Word of God and to faith. This truth was

imposed as a *criterion* on everything that also
claimed to be "religion" and to unite on terms
of equality with those great factors. In the history
of religions every really important reformation is
always, first and foremost, *a critical reduction*
to principles; for in the course of its historical
development, religion, by adapting itself to circumstances, attracts to itself much alien matter, and
produces, in conjunction with this, a number of
hybrid and apocryphal elements, which it is
necessarily compelled to place under the protection of what is sacred. If it is not to run wild
from exuberance, or be choked by its own dry
leaves, the reformer must come who purifies it and
brings it back to itself. This critical reduction to
principles Luther accomplished in the sixteenth
century, by victoriously declaring that the Christian
religion was given only in the Word of God and in
the inward experience which accords with this Word.

In the *second* place, there was the definite way
in which the "Word of God" and the "experience"
of it were grasped. For Luther the "Word" did
not mean Church doctrine; it did not even mean
the Bible; it meant the message of the free grace
of God in Christ which makes guilty and despairing men happy and blessed; and the "experience"
was just the certainty of this grace. In the sense
in which Luther took them, both can be embraced
in one phrase : *the confident belief in a God of
grace.* They put an end—such was his own ex-

perience, and such was what he taught—to all
inner discord in a man; they overcome the burden
of every ill; they destroy the sense of guilt; and,
despite the imperfection of a man's own acts, they
give him the certainty of being inseparably united
with the holy God:

> *Now I know and believe*
> *And give praise without end*
> *That God the Almighty*
> *Is Father and Friend,*
> *And that in all troubles,*
> *Whatever betide,*
> *He hushes the tempest*
> *And stands at my side.*

Nothing, he taught, is to be preached but the
God of Grace, with whom we are reconciled through
Christ. Conversely, it is not a question of ecstasies
and visions; no transports of feeling are necessary;
it is *faith* that is to be aroused. Faith is to be
the beginning, middle, and end of all religious
fervour. In the correspondence of Word and faith
"justification" is experienced, and hence justification
holds the chief place in the Reformers' message; it
means nothing less than the attainment of peace
and freedom in God through Christ, dominion over
the world, and an eternity within.

Lastly, the third feature of this renewal was the
great transformation which *God's worship* now inevitably underwent, God's worship by the individual and by the community. Such worship—

this was obvious—can and ought to be nothing
but putting *faith* to practical proof. As Luther
declared over and over again, "all that God asks
of us is faith, and it is through faith alone that
He is willing to treat with us." To let God be
God, and to pay Him honour by acknowledging
and invoking Him as Father — it is thus alone
that a man can serve Him. Every other path on
which a man tries to approach Him and honour
Him leads astray, and vain is the attempt to
establish any other relation with Him. What an
enormous mass of anxious, hopeful, and hopeless
effort was now done away with, and what a revolution in worship was effected ! But all that is
true of God's worship by the individual is true in
exactly the same way of public worship. Here, too,
it is only the Word of God and prayer which have
any place. All else is to be banished ; the community assembled for God's worship is to proclaim
the message of God with praise and thanksgiving,
and call upon His name. Anything that goes beyond this is not worship at all.

These three points embrace the chief elements in the
Reformation. What they involved was a *renewal* of
religion ; for not only do they denote, albeit in a
fashion of their own, a return to Christianity as it
originally was, but they also existed themselves in
Western Catholicism, although buried in a heap of
rubbish.

But, before we go further, permit me two brief

digressions. We were just saying that the community assembled for God's worship must not solemnise its worship in any other way than by proclaiming the Word and by prayer. To this, however, we must add, according to the Reformers' injunctions, that all that is to stamp this community as a Church is its existence as a community of the faith in which God's Word is preached aright. Here we may leave the sacraments out of account, as, according to Luther, they, too, derive their entire importance from the Word. But if Word and faith are the only characteristics of worship, it looks as if those who contend that the Reformation did away with the visible Church and put an invisible one in its place were right. But the contention does not tally with the facts. The distinction between a visible and an invisible Church dates back as far as the Middle Ages, or even, from one point of view, as far as Augustine. Those who defined the true Church as "the number of the predestined" were obliged to maintain that it was wholly invisible. But the German Reformers did not so define it. In declaring the Church to be a community of the faith in which God's Word is preached aright, they rejected all the coarser characteristics of a Church, and certainly excluded the visibility that appeals to the senses ; but—to take an illustration—who would say that an intellectual community, for example, a band of young

men all alike eagerly devoted to knowledge or the
interests of their country, was "invisible," because
it possesses no external characteristics, and cannot
be counted on one's fingers? Just as little is the
evangelical Church an "invisible" community. It
is a community of the spirit, and therefore its
"visibility" takes different phases and different
degrees of strength. There are phases of it where
it is absolutely unrecognisable, and others, again,
where it stands forth with the energy of a power
that appeals to the senses. It can never, indeed,
take the sharp contours of a State like the Vene-
tian republic or the kingdom of France—such was
the comparison which a great exponent of Catholic
dogmatics declared to be applicable to his Church
—but as Protestants we ought to know that we
belong, not to an "invisible" Church, but to a
spiritual community which disposes of the forces
pertaining to spiritual communities ; a spiritual
community resting on earth, but reaching to the
Eternal.

And now as to the other point : Protestantism
maintains that, objectively, the Christian community
is based upon the Gospel alone, but that the Gospel
is contained in Holy Scripture. From the very beginning it has encountered the objection that, if
that be so, and at the same time there be no recognised authority to decide what the purport and
meaning of the Gospel is and how it is to be ascertained from the Scriptures, general confusion will

be the result; that of this confusion the history of Protestantism affords ample testimony; that if every man has a warrant to decide what the "true understanding" of the Gospel is, and in this respect is bound to no tradition, no council, and no pope, but exercises the free right of research, any unity, community, or Church is absolutely impossible; that the State, therefore, must interfere, or some arbitrary limit be fixed. That no Church possessing the Sacred Office of the Inquisition can arise in this way is certainly true; further, that to impose any *external* limits on a community *from the inside* is a simple impossibility. What has been done by the State or under pressure of historical necessities does not affect the question at all; the structures which have arisen in the way are, in the evangelical sense, only figuratively called "Churches." *Protestantism reckons—* this is the solution—*upon the Gospel being something so simple, so divine, and therefore so truly human, as to be most certain of being understood when it is left entirely free, and also as to produce essentially the same experiences and convictions in individual souls.* In this it may often enough make mistakes; differences of individuality and education may issue in very heterogeneous results; but still, in this its attitude, it has not up to now been put to shame. A real, spiritual community of evangelical Christians; a common conviction as to what is most important and as to its application to life in all its forms, has arisen and is in full force and vigour. This community embraces Protestants in and outside Germany, Lutherans, Calvinists, and adherents of other denominations. In all of them, so far as they are earnest Christians, there lives a common element, and this element is of infinitely greater importance and value than all their differences. It keeps us to the Gospel and it protects us from modern heathenism and from relapse into Catholicism. More than this we do not need; nay, any other fetter we reject. This, however, is no fetter, but the condition of our freedom. And when we are reproached with our divisions and told that Protestantism has as many doctrines as heads, we reply, "So it has, but we do not wish it otherwise; on the contrary, we want still more freedom, still greater individuality in utterance and in doctrine; the historical circumstances necessitating the formation of national and free churches have imposed only too many rules and limitations upon us, even though they be not proclaimed as divine ordinances; we want still more confidence in the inner strength and unifying power of the Gospel, which is more certain to prevail in free conflict than under guardianship; we want to be a spiritual realm and we have no desire to return to the fleshpots of Egypt; we are well aware that in the interests of order and instruction outward and visible communities must arise; we are ready to foster their growth, so far as they fulfil these aims and deserve to be fostered; but we do not hang our hearts upon them, for they may exist to-day and to-morrow give place, under other political or social conditions, to new organisations; let anyone who has such a Church have it as though he had it not; our Church is not the particular Church in which we are placed, but the 'societas fidei' which has its members everywhere, even among Greeks and Romans." That is the evangelical answer to the reproach that we are "divided," and that is the language which the liberty that has been given to us employs. Let us now return from these digressions to the exposition of the essential features of Protestantism.

Protestantism was not only a Reformation but also a *Revolution*. From the legal point of view the whole Church system against which Luther revolted could lay claim to full obedience. It had just as much legal validity in Western Europe as the laws of the State themselves. When Luther burnt the papal bull he undoubtedly performed a revolutionary act—revolutionary, not in the bad sense of a revolt against legal ordinance which is also moral ordinance as well, but certainly in the sense of a violent breach with a given legal condition. It was against this state of things that the new movement was directed, and it was to the following chief points that its protest in word and deed extended. Firstly: It protested against the entire hierarchical and priestly system in the Church, demanded that it should be abolished, and abolished it in favour of a common priesthood and an established order formed on the basis of the congregation. What a range this demand had, and to what an extent it interfered with the previously existing state of things, cannot be told in a few sentences. To explain it all would take hours. Nor can we here show how the various arrangements actually took shape in the evangelical churches. That is not a matter of fundamental importance, but what is of fundamental importance is that the "divine" rights of the Church were abolished.

Secondly : It protested against all formal, external authority in religion; against the authority, therefore, of councils, priests, and the whole tradition of the Church. That alone is to be authority which shows itself to be such within and effects a deliverance ; the thing itself, therefore, the Gospel. Thus Luther also protested against the authority of the letter of the Bible ; but we shall see that this was a point on which neither he nor the rest of the Reformers were quite clear, and where they failed to draw the conclusions which their insight into fundamentals demanded.

Thirdly : It protested against all the traditional arrangements for public worship, all ritualism, and every sort of "holy work." As it neither knows nor tolerates, as we have seen, any specific form of worship, any material sacrifice and service to God, any mass and any works done for God and with a view to salvation, the whole traditional system of public worship, with its pomp, its holy and semi-holy articles, its gestures and processions, came to the ground. How much could be retained in the way of form for *æsthetic* or *educa-*

tional reasons was, in comparison with this, a question of entirely secondary importance.

Fourthly: It protested against Sacramentalism. Baptism and the Lord's Supper it left standing, as institutions of the primitive Church, or, as it might be, of the Lord himself; but it desired that they should be regarded either as symbols and marks by which the Christian is known, or as acts deriving their value exclusively from that message of the forgiveness of sins which is bound up with them. All other sacraments it abolished, and with them the whole notion of God's grace and help being accessible in bits, and fused in some mysterious way with definite corporeal things. To sacramentalism it opposed the *Word*, and to the notion that grace was given by bits, the conviction that there is only one grace, namely, to possess *God himself* as the source of grace. It was not because Luther was so very enlightened that in his tract "On the Babylonian Captivity" he rejected the whole system of Sacramentalism— he had enough superstition left in him to enable him to advance some very shocking contentions— but because he had had inner experience of the fact that where "grace" does not endow the soul with the living God Himself it is an illusion. Hence for him the whole doctrine of sacramentalism was an infringement of God's majesty and an enslavement of the soul.

Fifthly: It protested against the double form of morality, and accordingly against the higher form;

against the contention that it is particularly well-pleasing to God to make no use of the powers and gifts which are part of creation. The Reformers had a strong sense of the fact that the world passes away with the lusts thereof; we must certainly not represent Luther as the modern man cheerfully standing with his feet firmly planted on the earth; on the contrary, like the men of the Middle Ages he had a strong yearning to be rid of this world and to depart from the "vale of tears." But because he was convinced that we neither can nor ought to offer God anything but trust in Him, he arrived, in regard to the Christian's position in the world, at quite different theses from those which were advanced by the grave monks of previous centuries. As fastings and ascetic practices had no value before God, and were of no advantage to one's fellowmen, and as God is the Creator of all things, the most useful thing that a man can do is to remain in the position in which God has placed him. This conviction gave Luther a cheerful and confident view of earthly ordinances, which contrasts with and actually got the upperhand of his inclination to turn his back upon the world.

He advanced the definite thesis that all positions in life—constituted authority, the married state, and so on, down to domestic service—existed by the will of God, and were therefore genuinely spiritual positions in which we are to serve God; a faithful maidservant stands higher, with him, than a contemplative monk. Christians are not to be always devising how they may find some new paths of their own, but to show patience and love of neighbour within the sphere of their given vocation. Out of this there grew up in his mind the notion that all worldly laws and spheres of activity have an independent title. It is not that they are to be merely tolerated, and have no right to exist until they receive it from the Church. No! they have rights of their own, and they form the vast domain in which the Christian is to give proof of his faith and love; nay, they are even to be respected in places which are as yet ignorant of God's revelation in the Gospel.

It was thus that the same man who asked nothing of the world, so far as his own personal feelings were concerned, and whose soul was troubled only by thought for the Eternal, delivered mankind from the ban of asceticism. He was thereby really and truly the life and origin of a new epoch, and he gave it back a simple and unconstrained attitude towards the world, and a good conscience in all earthly labour. This fruitful work fell to his share, not because he secularised religion, but because he took it so seriously and so profoundly that, while in his view it was to pervade all things, it was itself to be freed from everything external to it.

LECTURE XVI.

THE question has often been raised whether, and to what extent, the Reformation was a work of the *German* spirit. I cannot here go into this complicated problem. But this much seems to me to be certain, that while we cannot, indeed, connect Luther's momentous religious experiences with his nationality, the results positive as well as negative with which he invested them display the German; the German man and German history. From the time that the Germans endeavoured to make themselves really at home in the religion handed down to them—this did not take place until the thirteenth century onwards—they were preparing the way for the Reformation. And just as Eastern Christianity is rightly called Greek, and the Christianity of the Middle Ages and of Western Europe is rightly called Roman, so the Christianity of the Reformation may be described as German, in spite of Calvin. For Calvin was Luther's pupil, and he made his influence most lastingly felt, not among the Latin nations but among the English, the Scotch, and the Dutch. Through the Reformation the Germans mark a stage in the history of the Universal Church. No similar statement can be made of the Slavs.

The recoil from asceticism, which as an ideal never penetrated the Germans to the same extent as other nations, and the protest against religion as external authority, are to be set down as well to the Pauline Gospel as to the German spirit. Luther's warmth and heartiness in preaching, and his frankness in polemical utterance, were felt by the German nation to be an opening out of its own soul.

In the previous lecture we touched upon the chief provinces in which Luther raised an emphatic and still effective protest. There is much upon which I could also dwell : for example, upon the opposition which, especially at the commencement of his reforming activity, he offered to the whole terminology of dogmatics, its formulæ and doctrinal utterances. To sum up : he protested, because his aim was to restore the Christian religion in its purity, without priests and sacrifices, without external authorities and ordinances, without solemn ceremonies, without all the chains with which the Beyond was to be bound to the Here. In its revising ardour the Reformation went back not only earlier than the eleventh century, not only earlier than the fourth or the second, but to the very beginnings of religion. Nay, without being aware of it, the Reformation even modified or entirely put aside forms which existed even in the apostolic age : thus in matters

of discipline it abolished fasting; in matters of
constitution it abolished bishops and deacons; in
matters of doctrine it abolished, among other things,
Chiliasm.

But with the change effected by Reformation and
Revolution, how does the new creation stand *as a
whole* in regard to the Gospel? We may say that
in the four leading points which we emphasised in
the previous lecture—inwardness and spirituality,
the fundamental thought of the God of grace, His
worship in spirit and in truth, and the idea of the
Church as a community of faith—the Gospel was in
reality re-won. Need I prove this in detail, or are
we to be shaken in our conviction because, as is
surely the case, a Christian in the sixteenth and in
the nineteenth century presents an appearance different from that which a Christian presented in
the first? That the inwardness and individualism
which the Reformation disengaged accord with the
character of the Gospel is certain. Further, Luther's
pronouncement on justification not only reflects in the
main, and in spite of certain irreducible differences,
Paul's train of thought, but is also in point of
aim in exact correspondence with Jesus' teaching.
To know God as one's Father, to possess a God of
grace, to find comfort in His grace and providence,
to believe in the forgiveness of sins—in both cases
that is the point on which everything turns. And
in the troubled times of Lutheran orthodoxy a Paul

Gerhardt succeeded in giving such grand expression
to this fundamental conviction of the Gospel in his
hymns, " Is God for me, then let all," and " Commit
thy ways," as to convince us how truly Protestantism was penetrated with it. Again, that the right
worship of God ought to be nothing but the acknowledgment of God in praise and prayer, but that the
love of neighbour is also worship, is taken direct
from the Gospel and Paul's corresponding injunctions.
Lastly, that the true Church is held together by the
Holy Ghost and by faith ; that it is a spiritual community of brothers and sisters, is a conviction which
is in line with the Gospel, and was most clearly
expressed by Paul. In so far as the Reformation re-
stored all this, and also recognised Christ as the only
Redeemer, it may in the strictest sense of the word
be called *evangelical*; and in so far as these convictions, crippled and burdened though they may be,
retain their ascendency in the Protestant Churches,
they have every warrant for being so described.

But what was here achieved had its dark side as
well. If we ask what the Reformation cost us, and
to what extent it made its principles prevail, we
shall see this dark side very clearly.

We get nothing from history without paying for
it, and for a violent movement we have to pay
double. What did the Reformation cost us ? I
will not speak of the fact that the unity of Western
civilisation was destroyed, since it was after all only

over a part of Western Europe that the Reformation
prevailed, for the freedom and many-sided character
of the resulting development brought us a greater
gain.   But the necessity of establishing the new
Churches as *State-Churches* was attended by serious
disadvantages.   The system of an ecclesiastical State
is, of course, worse, and its adherents have truly no
cause to praise it in contrast with the State-Churches.
But still the latter—which are not solely the outcome
of the breach with ecclesiastical authority, but were
already prepared for in the fifteenth century—have
been the cause of much stunted growth.   They have
weakened the feeling of responsibility, and diminished
the activity, of the evangelical communities ; and,
in addition, they have aroused the not unfounded
suspicion that the Church is an institution set up
by the State, and accordingly to be adjusted to the
State.   Much has happened, indeed, in the last
few decades to check that suspicion by the greater
independence which the Churches have obtained ;
but further progress in this direction is necessary,
especially in regard to the freedom of individual
communities.   The connexion with the State must
not be violently severed, for the Churches have
derived much advantage from it ; but steps must
be taken to further the development upon which
we have entered.   If this results in multifarious
organisations in the Church, it will do no harm ; on
the contrary, it will remind us, in a forcible way,
that these forms are all arbitrary.

Further, Protestantism was forced by its opposition to Catholicism to lay exclusive emphasis on the inward character of religion, and upon " faith alone " ; but to formulate one doctrine in sharp opposition to another is always a dangerous process. The man in the street is not sorry to hear that "good works " are unnecessary, nay, that they constitute a danger to the soul. Although Luther is not responsible for the convenient misunderstanding that ensued, the inevitable result was that in the reformed Churches in Germany from the very start there were accusations of moral laxity and a want of serious purpose in the sanctification of life. The saying " If ye love me, keep my commandments " was unwarrantably thrust into the background. Not until the Pietistic movement arose was its central importance once more recognised. Up till then the pendulum of the conduct of life took a suspicious swing in the contrary direction, out of opposition to the Catholic "justification by works." But religion is not only a state of the heart ; it is a deed as well, it is faith active in love and in the sanctification of life. This is a truth with which evangelical Christians must become much better acquainted, if they are not to be put to shame.

There is another point closely connected with what I have just mentioned. The Reformation abolished monasticism, and was bound to abolish it. It rightly affirmed that to take a vow of lifelong asceticism was a piece of presumption ; and it rightly considered

that any worldly vocation, conscientiously followed
in the sight of God, was equal to, nay, was better
than, being a monk. But something now happened
which Luther neither foresaw nor desired : "monasticism," of the kind that is conceivable and necessary in the evangelical sense of the word, disappeared
altogether. But every community stands in need of
personalities living *exclusively* for its ends. The
Church, for instance, needs volunteers who will
abandon every other pursuit, renounce "the world,"
and devote themselves entirely to the service of their
neighbour; not because such a vocation is "a higher
one," but because it is a necessary one, and because
no Church can live without also giving rise to this
desire. But in the evangelical Churches the desire
has been checked by the decided attitude which they
have been compelled to adopt towards Catholicism.
It is a high price that we have paid ; nor can the
price be reduced by considering, on the other hand,
how much simple and unaffected religious fervour
has been kindled in home and family life. We may
rejoice, however, that in the past century a beginning
has been made in the direction of recouping this loss.
In the institution of deaconesses and many cognate
phenomena the evangelical Churches are getting back
what they once ejected through their inability to
recognise it in the form which it then took. But
it must undergo a much ampler and more varied
development.

    Not only had the Reformation to pay a high price ;

it was also incapable of perceiving all the conclusions
to which its new ideas led, and of giving them pure
effect. It is not that the work which it did was not
absolutely valid and permanent in every particular—
how could that be, and who could desire it to have
been so ? No ! it remained stationary in its development even at the point at which, to judge by the
earnest foundation that was laid at the start, higher
things might have been expected. Various causes
combined to produce this result. From the year
1526 onwards national Churches had to be founded
at headlong speed on evangelical lines ; they were
forced to be " rounded and complete " at a time
when much was still in a state of flux. Then again,
a mistrust of the left wing, of the " enthusiasts,"
induced the Churches to offer an energetic resistance
to tendencies which they could have accompanied for
a good bit of their way. Luther's unwillingness to
have anything to do with them, nay, the manner in
which he became suspicious of his own ideas when
they coincided with those of the " enthusiasts," was
bitterly avenged and came home to the evangelical
Churches in the Age of Enlightenment. Even at the
risk of being reckoned among Luther's detractors, we
must go further. This genius had a faith as robust
as Paul's, and thereby an immense power over the
minds and hearts of men ; but he was not abreast
of the knowledge accessible even in his own time.
The *naïve* age had gone by ; it was an age of deep
feeling, of progress, an age in which religion could

not avoid contact with all the powers of mind. In this age it was his destiny to be forced to be not only a reformer but also an intellectual and spiritual leader and teacher. The way of looking at the world and at history he had to plan afresh for generations ; for there was no one there to help him, and to no one else would people listen. But he had not all the resources of clear knowledge at his command. Lastly, he was always anxious to go back to the original, to the Gospel itself, and, so far as it was possible to do it by intuition and inward experience, he did it ; moreover, he made some admirable studies in history, and in many places broke victoriously through the serried lines of the traditional dogmas. But any trustworthy knowledge of the history of those dogmas was as yet an impossibility, and still less was any historical acquaintance with the New Testament and primitive Christianity attainable. It is marvellous how in spite of all this Luther possessed so much power of penetration and sound judgment. We have only to look at his introductions to the books of the New Testament, or at his treatise on " Churches and Councils." But there were countless problems of which he did not even know, to say nothing of being able to solve them ; and so it was that he had no means of distinguishing between kernel and husk, between what was original and what was of alien growth. How can we be surprised, then, if in its doctrine, and in the view which it took of history, the Reformation was far from being a finished product ;

and that, where it perceived no problems, confusion in its own ideas was inevitable? It could not, like Pallas Athene, spring complete from Jupiter's head; as doctrine it could do no more than mark a *beginning*, and it had to reckon on future development. But by being rapidly formed into national Churches it came near to itself cutting short its further development for all time.

As regards the confusion and the checks which it brought upon itself, we must content ourselves with referring to a few leading points. Firstly, Luther would admit nothing but the Gospel, nothing but what frees and binds the consciences of men, what everyone, down to the man-servant and the maid-servant, can understand. But then he not only took the old dogmas of the Trinity and the two natures as part of the Gospel—he was not in a position to examine them historically—and even framed new ones, but he was absolutely incapable of making any sound distinction between " doctrine " and Gospel; in this respect falling far behind Paul. The necessary result was that intellectualism was still in the ascendant; that a scholastic doctrine was again set up as necessary to salvation; and that two classes of Christians once more arose : those who understand the doctrine, and the minors who are dependent on the others' understanding of it.

Secondly, Luther was convinced that that alone is the " Word of God " whereby a man is inwardly born anew—the message of the free grace of God in

Christ. At the highest levels to which he attained
in his life he was free from every sort of bondage
to the letter. What a capacity he had for distinguishing between law and Gospel, between Old and
New Testament, nay, for distinguishing in the New
Testament itself! All that he would recognise was
the kernel of the matter, clearly revealed as it is in
these books, and proving its power by its effect on
the soul. But he did not make a clean sweep. In
cases where he had found the letter important, he
demanded submission to the " it is written "; and he
demanded it peremptorily, without recollecting that,
where other sayings of the Scriptures were concerned,
he himself had declared the " it is written" to be
of no binding force.

Thirdly, grace is the forgiveness of sins, and therefore the assurance of possessing a God of grace, and
life, and salvation. How often Luther repeated this,
always with the addition that what was efficacious
here was the *Word*—that union of the soul with
God in the trust and childlike reverence which God's
Word inspires; it was a personal relation which was
here involved. But the same man allowed himself
to be inveigled into the most painful controversies
about the means of grace, about communion and
infant baptism. These were struggles in which he
ran the risk of again exchanging his high conception
of grace for the Catholic conception, as well as of
sacrificing the fundamental idea that it is a purely
spiritual possession that is in question, and that,

compared with Word and faith, all else is of no importance. What he here bequeathed to his Church has become a legacy of woe.

Fourthly, the counter-Church which, as was inevitable, rapidly arose in opposition to the Roman Church, and under the pressure which that Church exercised, perceived, not without reason, that its truth and its title lay in the re-establishment of the Gospel. But whilst the counter-Church privily identified the sum and substance of its doctrine with the Gospel, the thought also stole in surreptitiously : *We*, that is to say, the particular Churches which had now sprung up, *are the true Church.* Luther, of course, was never able to forget that the true Church was the sacred community of the faithful ; but still he had no clear ideas as to the relation between it and the visible new Church which had now arisen, and subsequent generations settled down more and more into the sad misunderstanding : We are the true Church *because we have the right doctrine.*" This misunderstanding, besides giving rise to evil results in self-infatuation and intolerance, still further strengthened that mischievous distinction between theologians and clergy on the one side, and the laity on the other, on which we have already dwelt. Not, perhaps, in theory, but certainly in practice, a double form of Christianity arose, just as in Catholicism ; and in spite of the efforts of the Pietistic movement, it still remains with us to-day. The theologian and the clergyman must defend the

whole doctrine, and be orthodox; for the layman
it suffices if he adheres to certain leading points and
refrains from attacking the orthodox creed. A very
well-known man, as I have been lately told, expressed
the wish that a certain inconvenient theologian
would go over to the philosophical faculty; "for
then," he said, "instead of an unbelieving theologian we should have a believing philosopher."
Here we have the logical outcome of the contention
that in the evangelical Churches, too, doctrine is
something laid down for all time, and that in spite
of being generally binding it is a matter of so much
difficulty that the laity need not be expected to
defend it. But if we persist on this path, and other
confusions become worse confounded and take firmer
root, there is a risk of Protestantism becoming a
sorry double of Catholicism. I say a sorry double,
because there are two things which Protestantism
will never obtain, namely, a pope and monastic
priests. Neither the letter of the Bible nor any
belief embodied in creeds can ever produce the
unconditional authority which Catholics possess in
the pope; and Protestantism cannot now return to
the monastic priest. It retains its national Churches
and its married clergy, neither of which looks very
stately by the side of Catholicism, if competition
with Catholicism is what the evangelical Churches
desire.

Gentlemen, Protestantism is not yet, thank God,
in such a bad way that the imperfections and con-

fusions in which it began have got the upperhand and entirely stunted or stifled its true character. Even those among us who are convinced that the Reformation in the sixteenth century is something that is over and done with are by no means ready to abandon the momentous ideas on which it was based, and there is a large field in which all earnest evangelical Christians are in complete unanimity. But if those who think that the Reformation is done with cannot see that its continuance in the sense of a pure understanding of God's Word is a question of life and death for Protestantism—its continuance has already borne abundant fruit in associations like the *Evangelical Union*—let them at least promote the liberty for which Luther fought in his best days: " Let the minds of men rush one against another and strike ; if some are meanwhile led astray—well ! that is what we must expect in war ; where there is battle and slaughter, some must fall and be wounded, but whoso fights honestly will receive the crown."

The reason why the catholicising of the Protestant Churches—I do not mean that they are becoming papal ; I mean that they are becoming Churches of ordinance, doctrine, and ceremony—is so burning a question is that three powerful forces are working together to further this development. First there is the indifference of the masses. The tendency of all indifference is to put religion on the same plane with authority and tradition, but

also with priests, hierarchies, and the cult of ceremonies. It puts religion there, and then goes on
to complain of the external character and stationary
condition of religion, and of the "pretensions" of the
clergy; nay, it is capable, apparently, at one and the
same moment, of mingling those complaints with
abuse, of contemptuously jeering at every active expression of religious feeling, and doing homage to
every kind of ceremony. This kind of indifference
has no understanding whatever for evangelical Christianity, instinctively tries to suppress it, and praises
Catholicism at its expense. The second of the
forces to be taken into consideration is what I
may call "natural religion." Those who live by
fear and hope; whose chief endeavour is to find
some authority in matters of religion; who are
eager to be rid of their own responsibility and
want to be reassured; who are looking for some
"adjunct" to life, whether in its solemn hours or
in its worst distress, some æsthetic transfiguration,
or some violent form of assistance till time itself
assists—all these people are also, without being
aware of it, putting religion on the Catholic plane;
they want "something that they can lean upon,"
and a good deal else, too—all kinds of things to
stir them up and help them; but they do not
want the Christianity of the Gospel. But the
Christianity of the Gospel in yielding to such
demands becomes Catholic Christianity. The third
force I mention unwillingly, and yet I cannot pass

it over in silence; it is the *State*. We must not blame the State for setting chief store by the conservative influence which religion and the Churches exercise, and the subsidiary effects which they produce in respect of reverence, obedience, and public order. But this is just the reason why the State exercises pressure in this direction, protects all the elements of stability in the Churches, and seeks to keep them from every inner movement that would call their unity and their " public utility " in question; nay, it has tried often enough to approximate the Church to the police, and employ it as a means of maintaining order in the State. We can pardon this—let the State take the means of power wherever it can find them; but the Church must not allow itself to be made into a pliant instrument; for, side by side with all the desolating consequences to its vocation and prestige, it would thereby become an outward institution in which public order is of greater consequence than the spirit, form more important than matter, and obedience of higher value than truth.

In the face of these three so different forces, what we have to do is to maintain Christian earnestness and liberty as presented in the Gospel. Theology alone is unavailing; what is wanted is firmness of Christian character. The evangelical Churches will be pushed into the background if they do not make a stand. It was out of such free creations as the Pauline communities were that the Catholic Church once arose. Who can guarantee that those Churches, too, will not become "Catholic" which had their origin in "the liberty of a Christian man"?

That, however, would not involve the destruction of the Gospel : so much, at least, history proves. It would be still traceable like a red thread in the centre of the web, and somewhere or other it would emerge afresh, and free itself from its entangling connexions. Even in the outwardly decorated but inwardly decayed temples of the Greek and Roman Church it has not been effaced. "Venture onwards! deep down in a vault you will still find the altar and its sacred, ever-burning lamp!" This Gospel, associated as it was with the speculative ideas and the mystery-worship of the Greeks, yet did not perish in them ; united with the Roman Empire, it held its own even in this fusion, nay, out of it gave birth to the Reformation. Its dogmatic doctrines, its ordinances of public worship, have changed ; nay, what is much more, it has been embraced by the simplest and purest minds and by the greatest thinkers ; it endeared itself to a St. Francis and to a Newton. It has outlived all the changing philosophies of the world ; it has cast off like a garment forms and ideas which were once sacred ; it has participated in the entire progress of civilisation ; it has become spiritualised, and in the course of history it has learnt how to make a surer application of its ethical principles. In its original earnestness and in the consolation which it offers, it has come home to thousands in all ages; and in all ages, too, it has thrown off all its encumbrances, and broken down all barriers. If we were right in saying that the Gospel is the knowledge and recognition of God as the Father, the certainty of redemption, humility and joy in God, energy and brotherly love; if it is essential to this religion that the founder must not be forgotten over his message, nor the message over the founder, history shows us that the Gospel has, in point of fact, remained in force, struggling again and again to the surface.

You will perhaps have felt that I have not entered into present questions, the relation, namely, of the Gospel to our present intellectual condition, our whole knowledge of the world, and our task therein. But to do this with any success in regard to the actual situation of affairs would require longer than a few flooting hours. As regards the kernel of the matter, however, I have said all that is needful, for no new phase in the history of the Christian Religion has occurred since the Reformation. Our knowledge of the world has undergone enormous changes—every century since the Reformation marks an advance, the most important being those in the last two; but, looked at from a religious and ethical point of view, the forces and principles of the Reformation have not been outrun or rendered obsolete. We need only grasp them in their purity

and courageously apply them, and modern ideas will
not put any *new* difficulties in their way.   The real
difficulties in the way of the religion of the Gospel
remain the old ones.   In face of them we can "prove"
nothing, for our proofs are only variations of our
convictions.   But the course which history has taken
has surely opened up a wide province, in which the
Christian sense of brotherhood must give practical
proof of itself quite otherwise than it knew how, or
was able, to do in the early centuries—I mean the
social province.   Here a tremendous task confronts
us, and in the measure in which we accomplish it
shall we be able to answer with a better heart
the deepest of all questions—*the question of the
meaning of life.*

Gentlemen, it is religion, the love of God and
neighbour, which gives life a meaning; knowledge
cannot do it.   Let me, if you please, speak of my
own experience, as one who for thirty years has
taken an earnest interest in these things.   Pure
knowledge is a glorious thing, and woe to the man
who holds it light or blunts his sense for it.   But
to the question, Whence, whither, and to what purpose, it gives an answer to-day as little as it did two
or three thousand years ago.   It does, indeed, in-
struct us in facts; it detects inconsistencies; it links
phenomena; it corrects the deceptions of sense and
idea.   But where and how the curve of the world
and the curve of our own life begin—that curve of

which it shows us only a section—and whither this
curve leads, knowledge does not tell us. But if with
a steady will we affirm the forces and the standards
which on the summits of our inner life shine out as
our highest good, nay, as our real self; if we are
earnest and courageous enough to accept them as
the great Reality and direct our lives by them; and
if we then look at the course of mankind's history,
follow its upward development, and search, in strenuous and patient service, for the communion of minds
in it, we shall not faint in weariness and despair, but
become certain of God, of the God whom Jesus Christ
called his Father, and who is also our Father.